Blueness of a Clear Sky

*Memoir of a Danube Swabian Refugee
and Her Journey to Healing*

Blueness of a Clear Sky

Memoir of a Danube Swabian Refugee
and Her Journey to Healing

Hildegard A. Weiler

Historical Background by Michelle Mouton, PhD
Prepared for publication by Marsha Rossiter, PhD

Monka Press, LLC

Published by
Monka Press, LLC
PO Box 2195
Oshkosh, Wisconsin 54903
Email: monkapress@yahoo.com

ISBN-13: 978-0615766409
ISBN-10: 0615766404
LCCN: 20133933191

Cover art by Hildegard A. Weiler, "Common Good" (2005).

Design and typesetting: HenschelHAUS Author Services

Printed in the United States of America.

Table of Contents

Editor's Notes

I met Hildegard Weiler only once, a few months before her death in 2009. I was introduced to Hildie and to her book manuscript by her sister, my friend, Hedi Weiler. Over the course of a weekend in Charlotte, North Carolina, I visited with Hildie about her hopes and plans for this book. I recorded several of our conversations, in which she spoke about her childhood experiences and about her intentions for the manuscript. In the end, she entrusted the manuscript to me for further editing and publication. Following her instructions, I completed a rewrite of the manuscript in order to bring the full story into a first-person, present-tense account of her wartime experiences. I also completed, from her notes and comments, the scenes with her psychiatrist, which serve as lead-ins to each of the chapters. She had begun this rewriting prior to the final stages of her illness, but was not able to bring it to completion.

It was Hildie's hope that the publication of this work would bring attention to the impact of war and violence on children. It was *not* her intention to write an historical account of World War II or the plight of the *Donauschwaben* in Hungary or the political complexities of the Balkan region during that period. It *was* her aim to bring the reader into a child's experience of being a war refugee by telling her story from the point of view of her seven-year-old self. Her decision to write her experiences from her childhood perspective proved to be a powerful technique. As readers of her story, we—like seven-year-old Hildie—are sometimes confused and lost. We do not always know where the scenes take place, or why. But as we are captivated and touched by the intensity of Hildie's experience, we are drawn into her narrative.

To assist the reader in understanding the historical, political, and geographical contexts of Hildie's experience, I have included an introductory *Historical Background* section prepared by Dr. Michelle Mouton, a faculty member in the history department at the University of Wisconsin Oshkosh. I am most grateful to Professor Mouton for sharing her knowledge of the region and the period to enhance readers' understanding of the events described. I have also included a map that depicts the areas in which Hildie's story takes place.

Parallel with the recounting of her childhood episodes, Hildie included scenes from her therapeutic sessions with psychiatrist, Dr. Gregg. This is a unique contribution of Hildie's book—the juxtaposition of her descriptions of her childhood wounding with her healing as an adult. The result is a powerful story that offers insight into recovery from post-traumatic stress disorder.

I want to call the reader's attention to the theme of light that is ever-present throughout Hildie's book. Images of light are frequent in her story. The drops of rain on the bushes shining in the sunlight, the distant rectangle of sun in the top of the box car or bomb shelter, the light that gleams at the end of a train tunnel—these and many more images lead us to an appreciation of the symbolic importance of light and its sustaining power in Hildie's life. In her words, "I survived because of an inner determination not to give up. Most powerful were the images of light that touched my soul. However we interpret their meaning, the fact remains that in my darkest hours in the bunkers and on the trains, the healing rays of sun reached out and kept me sane in a world gone mad."

Several individuals have offered assistance and guidance to me as I have worked with Hildie's manuscript, and I want to acknowledge them here. Katherine Thompson of the Wisconsin Historical Society Press, Dr. John M. Michels, Dr. Susan Clarkson, and Lee Rossiter all read the manuscript and each offered valuable feedback to me on its final preparation. I am most grateful to them.

I extend heartfelt thanks to members of Hildie's family for their support and patience throughout this process. Hedwig Weiler,

Hildie's sister and my dear friend, has lovingly encouraged my work on this project from the beginning. The *Epilogue in Three Voices* includes commentaries by Hedi, and also by Susan Klemm Slaughter and Kenneth Joseph Klemm, Hildie's daughter and son. These are the people who knew Hildie best. Each offers a unique perspective on Hildie's adult life. I thank them for their contributions.

Finally, I want to say that it has been a privilege and honor for me to work with Hildie's manuscript and to help bring it to publication. From time to time, life brings to each of us gifts of learning, gifts of insight. For me, the invitation by Hildie to work with her story was such a gift. For that, I am deeply grateful.

Marsha Rossiter

Historical Background

In 1945, responsibility for the Second World War was laid squarely at the hands of the Germans and their then dead leader, Adolf Hitler. The subsequent revelation of the horrors that had been committed by the Nazis and the vast destruction of much of Europe in pursuit of Hitler's dream, complicated Germans' ability to describe their own suffering. In recent years the publication of several different kinds of histories has created a new space in the public mind for the consideration of the suffering of German people as a result of the Second World War.

First, several books delved into the horrific experience of German civilians who lived through the Allied bombings.[1] Second, studies of Eastern Europeans (especially from Poland and East Prussia) began to recount the brutal treatment suffered by ethnic Germans as they were expelled from Eastern Europe at the end of the Second World War.[2] Third, as the generation that experienced the war and its aftermath faces the end of their lives, an increasing number of elder Germans are telling their stories. As a result, a new and growing number of autobiographies have been published.[3] This book is the account of a young ethnic German girl's experience of being expelled from South Eastern Europe. As such, Hildie's memoir contributes a valuable new voice to the latter two of these bodies of literature.

Hildie's memoir is unusual in that she grew up not in Poland, from whence most refugee accounts originate, but among the *Donauschwaben* Germans, who lived in Hungary, Yugoslavia, and Romania. Here a bit of historical background will be helpful to the reader. During the seventeenth century, the Habsburg Empire sent the *Donauschwaben* Germans to populate and civilize the lands recently acquired from the Ottoman Empire. With no roads, they traveled down the Danube River (or *Donau*, in German) on barges to settle in villages where most farmed. For the most part they lived peacefully with the local populations, sometimes integrating themselves into local customs, politics, and economics, and at other times, remaining separate. Conflict though not unknown, was infrequent.

The First World War changed life for the *Donauschwaben* Germans in Eastern Europe. President Woodrow Wilson's Fourteen Points, which served as the basis for peace, called for the self-determination of all peoples. This resulted in the Treaty of Trianon, signed with Hungary in 1920, which reduced Hungary's borders by 72 percent and its population by 64 percent. The peace treaties also created Czechoslovakia and Yugoslavia, two countries which reflected the optimistic belief present in 1918 that ethnic groups could live together in peace. When the Habsburg Empire fell in 1918, 1.5 million Germans lived in the three successor states: Hungary, Romania, and Yugoslavia.

The First World War ushered in a new nationalist spirit especially among the new states in Eastern Europe. The *Donauschwaben* and other Germans in Eastern Europe found that the aftermath of the war led to a new ethnic, national, and religious repression of minority groups. Germans in Eastern Europe responded by closing in on themselves, but found little protection from local anti-minority attitudes. As a result, some of these Germans, who had formerly supported liberal-conservative political parties or had been apolitical, became sympathetic to narrower right-wing, nationalist political views. This made them more receptive, if not supportive, of National Socialism when Hitler rose to power in 1933.

Hitler came to power in Germany on a nationalist, racial platform. He believed that the Germans were the "Aryan" Master Race. After six years of brutally cleansing the "unworthy" in Germany, he launched the Second World War to expand the

Lebensraum (living space) for the Master Race. Throughout Eastern Europe, he invaded and conquered. His conquest was not only a military conquest, however, it was also an ideological conquest based on his belief that the Eastern Europeans were an inferior [*minderwertig*] race to the Germans.

Throughout Eastern Europe, non-Germans were brutally mistreated on a spectrum which began with slave labor and ended with murder (especially of the Jews). The Nazis ignored numerous international treaties as prisoners of war were killed or left to die by the hundreds of thousands and civilians were raped and murdered. Nazi brutality profoundly affected Eastern European attitudes toward their former German neighbors, who had previously been greeted with tolerance if not full acceptance. The Nazi attitudes of racial superiority and military violence bred intolerance and hatred of even those German minorities who did not support the Nazis. By the end of the war, most Eastern Europeans felt the experiment in ethnic blending had failed and were determined to create homogenous nation-states.

Strong anti-Bolshevik propaganda produced by the Nazis together with even a rudimentary knowledge of the crimes perpetrated by the Nazis in Eastern Europe caused Germans to fear Stalin's Red Army. As the war turned against the Germans in the East and the Red Army advanced on Germany, well over six million Germans fled west. The Nazi leadership's insistence that Germany would ultimately prevail on the battlefront prevented the preparation of a realistic evacuation plan for ethnic Germans in the East. As a result, after it was already too late, ethnic German civilians in Eastern Europe fled West on trains, bikes, military transports, and on foot, carrying their livelihoods and clinging to their loved ones. What would inevitably have been a complicated process became utterly chaotic and deadly for many.

Hildie's account begins as she watches hour after hour as friends and neighbors trek by her grandparents' house on their way west. Her mother, like many Germans in Hungary, believed that she was safe and fled only at the last minute at the persistent behest of the German military.

Hildie's family initially arrived in Vienna, but were later moved through many different refugee camps in difficult locations. But even reaching Germany did not ensure an end to the troubles ethnic German refugees faced. As Hildie describes, the refugees were greeted with chilly stares by locals who were consumed with their own problems: avoiding bombs, finding food, and worrying about their husbands, fathers, and sons at war. No one was enthusiastic about taking in the impoverished and often traumatized refugees. Many refugees, like Hildie's mother, resented the way that locals treated them as uneducated (because of their dialect) or as Gypsies (because they were from Hungary) rather than as the successful middle-class Germans they were. Furthermore, as Richard Bessel has pointed out in *Germany 1945: From War to Peace*, the fact that "so many refugees regarded the loss of their *Heimat,* or homeland, as temporary, and did not imagine that they would have to build a new existence in their new communities, did nothing to make the processes of integration easier."[4]

When the war finally ended, many of the ethnic German refugees who had reached Germany wanted to leave Germany and go back home. Germany itself was divided between the American, Soviet, British, and French zones of occupation. The Soviets occupied the eastern zone and were quickly overwhelmed by refugees from Eastern Europe. To cope with this problem, they tried to shunt refugees to the western occupation zones, and periodically closed their own borders, leaving the refugees in camps along the border. When they were unable to feed the people in the refugee camps, however, they sent many back east to the regions from which they had fled. As one historian has pointed out, the Soviets "eased their own burden by sending the people on an absurd trip into the unknown."[5]

Policy also played a large role in the experiences of Germans in Eastern Europe. As the Second World War turned against the

Germans, the Big Three—Winston Churchill, Josef Stalin, and Franklin Roosevelt—met and discussed the future of Germany and Europe. Their insistence on unconditional surrender meant that they could design the contours of peace. At the Yalta Conference in February 1945, they agreed to punish the Germans for the unprecedented destruction they had inflicted on Europe and the world and to divide Germany and Berlin into occupation zones. Simultaneously, but less well-known, they debated how to draw the national boundaries in Central Europe in the aftermath of German occupation. Stalin insisted that the western Soviet border adhere to the Curzon line as he and Hitler had agreed in 1939.

At the Potsdam Conference in July 1945, the Western Allies confirmed Stalin's right to eastern Poland. In practical terms, this meant designating a large part of eastern Poland as Soviet territory. To compensate the Poles, the Allies moved Poland's western border into formerly German territory in the west. Borders in southeastern Europe were also adjusted as the Soviet Union and Yugoslavia expanded to include the region where Hildie's grandparents lived.

The Allies acknowledged the desire and right of Eastern Europeans to remove the Germans (former oppressors) from their countries. The *Sudeten* Germans, citizens of Czechoslovakia in the interwar period, had aided Hitler in taking over Czechoslovakia (and in many cases, contributed to its destruction during the war). This fraught past extinguished any hope that Czechoslovakians might continue to live peacefully with their former German neighbors. Similarly Poland and Yugoslavia sought to expel their German populations. The Allies did insist, however, that the expulsions were to take place in an "orderly and humane way."

On November 21, 1945, the Allied control declared that Germans who remained in Poland, Czechoslovakia, or Hungary could be sent west to Germany. They anticipated that this would result in 15 million Germans coming to Germany; it sparked a wave of state-enforced expulsions that could hardly be called "humane." To encourage the Germans to leave voluntarily, policies were enacted to make their lives increasingly difficult: they were robbed, denied food and medical care, excluded from school and work, and in many cases, women were raped. Simultaneously, any sign of German culture in public life was removed.

The expulsion of the ethnic Germans from Hungary was tightly connected to the land reform instituted by the Hungarian Communists and Nationalists. The only way to provide land to land-hungry Hungarians was to take it from the *Donauschwaben* landowners. As the Minister of Rebuilding, Joszef Antalls, said in a Cabinet Meeting on 22 December 1946: "It is in Hungary's best interest to force as many Germans as possible out of the country. There will never again be an opportunity like this one to get rid of Germans."[6] The expulsions began in January 1946 in the areas along the Austrian border where the *Donauschwaben* were living in cramped quarters. The revenge that the Hungarians felt toward the Germans reflected not their experience as an occupied country — as in the case of Poland and Czechoslovakia — but rather their frustration as former allies of the Germans, who had lost the war.

Hildie and her family discovered the wave of anti-German sentiment prevalent in postwar Eastern Europe as they began their trek back home. They could not return directly to Hilde's grandparent's house as they had planned because it had been incorporated into Yugoslavia, and the borders were closed to Germans. Instead, they stayed with her mother's friends in Hungary. Although the friends were kind and shared what they had with Hildie's family, life was difficult. They were able to survive by selling on the black market the parcels her grandparents sent from their farm in Yugoslavia. Even so, their poverty was dire enough that Hildie's mother decided to smuggle Hildie to her grandparents in Yugoslavia where she was sure the food would be sufficient.

Yugoslavia was not easy to enter, however. The trip was treacherous. In addition, between 1943 and November 1944, the "Antifascist Council of the People's Free Yugoslavia" had begun to dispossess and intern the ethnic Germans in Yugoslavia. The

Antifascist Council declared the Germans collectively guilty of Nazi crimes and therefore responsible for the war. Overnight, the Germans lost all their rights in Yugoslavia. The partisans exacted further revenge on the Germans during "Bloody Fall," when many Germans were killed.

Before the Second World War, 540,000 ethnic Germans like Hildie lived in Hungary. When the war ended, there were 195,000 *Donauschwaben* under Yugoslavian rule, most of them in forced labor camps. Hildie's grandfather managed to keep his family safe during this dangerous time. In the end, the family's American citizenship enabled them to get visas to immigrate to the United States. Hildie's story offers its readers a vivid account of one ethnic German girl's travails in postwar Eastern Europe.

Michelle Mouton, Ph.D.
Department of History
University of Wisconsin Oshkosh

Notes

[1] Jörg Friedrich, *The Fire: the Bombing of Germany 1941-1945* (New York: Columbia University Press, 2008); Hans Erich Nossack, *The End: 1943* (Chicago: University of Chicago Press, 2006).

[2] Andreas Kossert, *Kalte Heimat* (Munich: Siedler Verlag, 2008), Thomas Urban, *Der Verlust: Die Vertreibung der Deutschen und Polen im 20.Jahrhundert* (Munich: C.H. Beck, 2006), Guido Knopp, *Die grosse Flucht: Das Schicksal der Vertriebenen* (Munich: Ullstein Verlag, 2002); Norman Naimark, *Fires Of Hatred: Ethnic Cleansing In 20th Century Europe* (Harvard, 2001).

[3] Among the best are: Hans-Burkhard Sumowski, "Jetzt war ich ganz allein auf der Welt: Erinnerungen an eine Kindheit in Königsberg" *1944-1947* (München: Random House, 2009) and Ursula Mahrendorf, *The Shame of Survival: Working Through a Nazi Childhood* (University Park: Pennsylvania State Press, 2009).

[4] Richard Bessel, *Germany 1945: From War to Peace*, (New York: Harper Perennial, 2009), 91.

[5] Andreas Kossert, *Kalte Heimat*, 30. (Translation from the German by Michelle Mouton).

[6] Quoted in Andreas Kossert, *Kalte Heimat*, 38.

Map of Europe with Locations of Experiences Described in the Book

North
Sea

GREAT
BRITAIN

London

HOLLAND

BELGIUM

Rhine River

WEST

EISENBERG

SCHLEUSINGEN

CHEM

Berli

EAST

GERMA

LE HAVRE

Seine

PARIS

River

LUX

GERMANY

Danube River

FRANCE

SWITZERLAND

AU

ITALY

European Political Boundaries in 1937

SUDETENLAND

CZECHOSLOVAKIA

POLAND

RUTHENIA

AUSTRIA

HUNGARY

RUMANIA

SOMBOR
MILETITSCH

YUGOSLAVIA

River

Mediterranean Sea

Hildie born in Sombor on July 11, 1937.

Prologue

---

*W*hen I was a child, the elders told me the history of our people, which began over two hundred and fifty years ago in Germany when kings and queens owned all of the land. In exchange for safety, the people swore allegiance to the monarchy. The promise of free land in a distant region gave the commoners courage as they walked the many miles following the Danube River. The people became known as the *Donauschwaben*, or Danube Swabians. The resettlement, in what is now known as the Balkans in Serbia, served the purpose of being the first line of defense against invading hordes. A legend about this area tells that the new frontier was settled where Attila the Hun's army used to sit by their campfires under a star-studded sky. Of course, it is the nature of legends to present unverifiable facts, but I like to believe this reference to Attila the Hun is true because this connection to the past enriches my understanding of the present, and of who I am.

Many died in this strange, swampy land. But my ancestors were a hearty race. They buried their dead and carried on their work to drain the land and produce crops. After many generations, this land became bountiful with wheat, oats, and corn. Life remained basically unchanged until the mid-20th century.

~ ~ ~ ~ ~ ~

I was born in 1937 in the city of Zombor, which was then located in Hungary. Like the rest of my family, I spoke German and followed German customs.

My fondest memories are of visiting my grandparents in the little farming town of Miletitsch. In front of my grandparents' house were majestic walnut trees neatly planted in rows along the precisely laid brick sidewalk. On the other side of these magnificent trees was a ditch where rainwater flowed. A little higher, next to the ditch, was the road. It was unpaved—made of the same rich earth that these resourceful people made so bountiful.

In summer, clouds of dust rose as people walked and rode to the market and as sheep, geese, or cows were herded to the green pastures surrounding the town. When it rained, the road was so deep with mud that the horses were often unable to pull the wagons. Cursing loudly, big sweating men would push the metal-rimmed wooden wagon wheels out of the sucking mud. Ah, but when it snowed, all was quiet except for the whisper of sleigh runners and the rhythmic sound of muffled horses' hooves.

Vacations in this little town were a fairyland for a little girl from the city of Zombor. There was so much freedom to roam, and so many fascinating customs. Most of the farmwomen and girls still dressed in traditional clothes. Hand-knitted woolen shoes of lively floral patterns were sewn to pieces of leather that were cut around the bare feet for accurate sizing. On Sundays, the unmarried young farm women wore five or six heavily starched, mini-pleated white underskirts. The top skirt was of a fine black or dark blue material patterned with vivid green-stemmed red or pink flowers.

Special clothing was designated for each of the first three Sundays of the month. For example, on the first Sunday, all the women worshippers might wear skirts patterned with tiny flowers. On the next Sunday, they would wear patterns of big blotchy bunches of roses, and on the third, they might all wear dresses with blue embroidered silk flowers. On the fourth Sunday, they wore whatever they wished.

All the women braided their long hair into intricate patterns on the top of their heads. The dipped their combs into a sugar and water solution to smooth and hold a seven-part braid that resembled the bottom of an inverted small basket. A black velvet bow surrounded the gleaming circular creation as they proudly walked to Catholic mass.

During the week they wore dark brown, black, or navy blue crisply starched, cotton, floor-length skirts and aprons. On top, they wore matching tightly fitting jackets. The younger women usually wore material that was conservatively dotted. When a woman became 30 years of age, she started wearing a dark babushka every day of her life. At that time, when I was a child, only about a third of the women in town had traded their traditional somber clothes for the brightly colored simpler dresses worn by women in the city.

~ ~ ~ ~ ~ ~

The tumultuous events of the Second World War destroyed my youthful view of life. For more than two years, my mother, sister, and I were refugees in war-torn Europe, mostly in Germany. The events of that time etched themselves on my mind in a mosaic of confusion, terror, chaos, despair, fatigue — and sometimes also Light, gentleness, and love.

This memoir covers a span of approximately two years, beginning when I was seven years of age. My experiences from August 1944 to September 1946 started at home in Hungary before I fled with my mother and sister to escape the advancing Russian army. We traveled through Hungary, Czechoslovakia, and Austria to Germany. There we encountered the last stages of brutal conflict, where civilians and refugees were bombed day and night. The uncertainty and danger continued after World War II ended, and peace eluded our family until our arrival in the United States in autumn of 1946.

~ ~ ~ ~ ~ ~

After the war, our way of dealing with those horrors was not to speak of them. We retreated into silence so that we could focus on learning how to assimilate in America, speak the language, and become financially secure in our newly chosen home. Within this circle of silence, I survived with fear as my constant companion. But the source of the fear was a mystery to me.

In my late forties, I started having flashbacks that I could only describe as blank spaces filled with fear, panic, and anxiety. I feared for the sanity of my mind. For eighteen months, I worked with a psychiatrist to understand the flashbacks to my childhood experiences during the war years. Reliving each fearful experience took courage, but I could no longer bear the heavy burden of pain and panic from those childhood years. In time, I learned to recognize the onset of a flashback and to put it aside, now knowing that I was no longer the little girl filled with despair walking through bombed-out streets.

While in therapy, I recorded my childhood memories and experiences. This book is a compilation of those memories, woven into a narrative of my refugee experience. I have written about the war from a child's perspective as recalled by my adult self. Only an adult can truly comprehend the many layers of the physical, psychological, spiritual, emotional, and political effects of such traumatic experiences. Sometimes I took creative liberties for the sake of cohesion and continuity as I knitted my memories together, but I have made every effort to remain true to my experience.

Nevertheless, it sometimes seems impossible to truly distinguish fact from fiction. For the most part, the real names of the people in this story have been retained. My family and the families of those who died have given permission to use actual names. In the instances where references to names and exact locations may cause danger or personal discomfort, changes were made to protect them without drastically altering the experiences. If my insensitivity hurts any person mentioned in this book, I apologize.

I write these memories of this time of war as a legacy to future generations, so that some connections to that past will be known. It was a sad time in history; I pray that it will never be repeated. Also, I write to share how in my adult years, I healed psychologically with the help of a psychiatrist, and with the guidance of a loving spiritual presence from within. Writing this book was a healing catharsis for me. May this book bring hope to children in the 21st century.

Hildegard A. Weiler
(1937 – 2009)

Part 1

Before the War
Miletitsch and Zombor

Chapter One

"*Why are you here?" asks the psychiatrist, Dr. Gregg.*

"Something is happening to my mind. I...I... maybe I'm losing my mind," I stammer, sitting on the edge of the chair, my back ramrod straight, hands clasped on my lap, feet firmly planted on the wooden floor.

"Can you describe this more?"

"Sometimes my mind goes blank and I am in great fear, anxiety, and panic...rapid breathing."

"Do you know what precipitates these episodes?" his brown eyes totally focused on me.

"No, not really. I do know it has something to do with my childhood experiences during World War II, but I have no idea what is causing these effects on my mind."

"Why would the war have such an effect on you? Was your father in the military?"

"Well, yes. My father was in the German army." I pause. "I was born in Hungary — the part that is now Serbia. My mother, sister, and I were refugees for over two years in Europe — mostly in Germany — from 1944 to 1946, when we came to America."

We are both silent. I study him and the room. He must be in his fifties, graying, of medium build. He sits across from me on a brown leather chair; behind him, French doors open to sun dappled lush green gardens. This must be the living room of a large home. Dark brown paneled walls and built-in bookcases give the room a solid feeling. Lovely, thick, brightly colored, intricately patterned rugs are scattered on highly polished parquet floors. I am uncertain if this is where I can be healed.

"Are these episodes new?" he asks.

"I guess the fear and panic have been pretty much with me since the war, but more so now. My blank-mind episodes are fairly new, maybe a year or a little bit more. I think this started a few months before moving here to Shreveport," my eyes bore into him.

"Where did you move from? Why?"

"My husband works for AT&T. He was transferred from Chicago. We have been in Shreveport around nine months."

Again silence.

"Have you served in the military?" I query. "Vietnam? Korea?"

"No wars, but I have worked with a number of veterans."

My first session with Dr. Gregg ends. At home I am in a terrible state of uncertainty whether he is the person to help me. To me he seemed confrontational, almost brusque in his interactions with me. I desperately need help. Throughout the week, before my next session with him, I try to center myself in meditation as best I can, with my never-ending mantra, "God, help me, please help me God." How I miss the silent worship of my Quaker friends in Illinois and their gentle listening and counsel. I gain some comfort by holding myself in the Light, which is an old Quaker way of saying that I prayed for myself.

By my next appointment, I have made up my mind.

"I came back to tell you that I cannot work with you."

He seems surprised. "Why do you think that?"

"I have given this a lot of thought this past week. Since you have never been in a war, it just seems to me that you can never truly understand what happens — the wounding — of people during war, especially children."

Before I lose my courage, I rapidly blurt out, "And, your interactions with me feel confrontational and brusque."

"You feel that I am confrontational? In what way?" His voice sounds incredulous.

"I don't really know. I just know that you make me feel like I am being attacked – that what I have to say sounds bizarre or crazy. And that feeling makes it impossible for me to search for understanding. I need kindness and gentleness. I need to feel safe. . . . To feel that you . . . ," I trail off weakly.

We talk back and forth. He is very persuasive and warily I agree to try one or two more sessions with him. He assures me that he does know how to help me. Somehow I want to believe him, but I have misgivings. I know that I am in desperate need of help. I feel so alone…this feeling is very familiar.

The next week, with all of my defenses fortifying me, I return to Dr. Gregg. My pounding heart feels like it's banging against my rib cage. To slow my rapid breathing, I force myself to take deep breaths. My usual mantra has not left my heart and mind for one moment: "God help me. God. God. Help me."

My innate sense of self-preservation, a sort of stubbornness, deep freezes my emotions. This detached calmness has always protected me in frightening situations. We face each other, both of us on brown leather winged chairs.

"I'm glad you came back," he smiles gently.

Tears sting my eyes. Hoarsely I whisper, "Yes, I'm here," wringing my hands, taking deep breaths.

"Was it hard for you to come here today?"

Not trusting my voice, I nod.

He continues, "Never feel that you must do anything here in this room that you do not want to. You make the decision as to what you want to talk about. Is there something you want to talk about today?"

Much to my surprise, I recount the agony of this past week in deciding whether or not to keep my word to come to this session. I go on and on and on describing my ambivalence and fears for my sanity.

Without consciously noticing, there is a tiny crack in my carefully constructed frozen emotions.

At the end of the session I feel better. I have a sense of peace, but I am deeply fatigued. In the weekly sessions that follow, I talk about mundane details of my life while he gains my trust by not backing me into an emotional/psychological corner with brusque questions. Although I stick to the safety of glossing over my life, he and I both know that the war is the elephant in the room. His supportive comments become a life raft in my churning fearful emotions, which I believe are hidden from him. I am not ready to talk about the war.

I continue to scrutinize him as I share experiences of my life in the present, but increasingly, of my past. Sometimes I notice him taking a deep breath while shifting his body, opening and closing his mouth; I conclude that he is holding back confrontational words. His self-control reassures me. When I share a feeling or thought that is deep from my heart that could be seen as bizarre, or at least strange, he validates that I am well.

He encourages me to walk through painful experiences from those early childhood years. I sob and shudder, "I can't go back. It hurts too much. There must be another way. I cannot do it." He gives me a box of white tissues to dab my tears.

"Hildie, you have come this way by yourself...your memories are very close to the surface, which is good. But, you decide when you want to stop," he calms me.

Inch by inch, I trust him more.

He continues, "This is the way to heal what you call episodes of your blank mind. They are also referred to as flashbacks. You can do it, but you will make all decisions of where to go and when to stop. You are in total control. I will be with you — you will not be alone this time."

I struggle with accepting the process of reliving the horrors of war as a child. I weigh the possibility of just going on with my life and denying my fears as I have always done before. Yet, I know that I cannot continue to live in this overwhelming fear of what is happening to my mind.

I burst out loudly, "Surely at this stage of my life those memories should not be plaguing me so profoundly. For heaven's sake, I'm approaching my fiftieth birthday."

"The mind is complex. It's impossible to predict with any certainty what effect childhood experiences have on an adult. But, you can have greater understanding and, with that, healing of your experiences."

Squeezing my hands into white-knuckle fists, I gather all my courage to step into the swiftly moving swirling stream of black water, letting myself be led by a force greater than I, into the Unknown. I hope that I will survive. I let myself remember, "The war started for me when I was seven years old."

~~~~~~~

*W*earing a dress covered with tiny, brightly colored flowers, Grandmother stands in the entrance to the house, which is in the small farming town of Miletitsch in Hungary. She is standing on the highly polished black marble stairs of a narrow doorway. Next to the entrance is a mammoth wooden double door that opens for wagons heavily laden with fragrant, newly mowed hay from the fields, which is carefully unloaded and stored for winter in the stables for horses and cows.

Resting one hand on her petite hip and the other shielding her squinting eyes, she peers past the rows of tall walnut trees, past the drainage ditch that carries rainwater away from the road. An endless stream of people walking on the dirt road stirs up clouds of dust. Lips pursed, her eyebrows pulled together form two lines in the middle of her forehead.

"*Grossmutter, Grossmutter*," I, a blue-eyed, seven-year-old girl, ask anxiously, tugging on the flowered dress. "Where are all the people going?"

Grandmother answers distractedly, "They're going away, Hildie."

"But where, *Grossmutter?*" I persist.

"Just away, they don't know where."

I try to understand, sensing that something unusual is happening. I often visit my grandparents in Miletitsch and love the peaceful freedom of this farming community, which is so different from the city of Zombor where I live. Now the adults are strangely quiet.

Beyond my grandparents, in front of the house on the neat brick sidewalk, stands my cousin Theresa, a slender 17-year old girl. Her usually friendly face is also strained as she stares into the dust, which engulfs the streams of people.

Next to Theresa is her brother, Nicky, a tall, lanky boy of 14. Anxiously, he searches our Grandfather's quiet and reassuringly calm face. Grandfather places his hand on the boy's shoulder. The older man is tall despite the outward curve of his left leg caused by an injury long ago. His other hand resting on his hip, he appears to be calmly observing the movements on the road, but I notice his penetrating stare pierces the crowds and little lines deepen around his eyes.

Suddenly, Grandmother runs into the dusty road to a woman whose head is covered with a black babushka. Murmuring to each other, they embrace, choking back tears. The woman wipes her sweaty, grimy face with her black apron, then hurries to rejoin her family further down the road.

All are leaving countries where Germans settled centuries ago, walking through Hungary, Czechoslovakia, and Austria to Germany, where they hope to find safety from the approaching Russian army. The young men are at war fighting with the German army, leaving old men, women of all ages, and children walking along the road. Some in the never-ending stream of people are riding on horse-drawn wagons piled high with clanging cooking pots, down quilts, and the necessities of staying alive. Some are pushing or pulling sturdy carts filled with little children lulled into merciful sleep by the steady movement. Those without wagons or carts carry their precious possessions bundled up and tied to their backs. Young mothers carry babies on their hips holding the hands of siblings, whose tired little feet keep walking, walking....

Greetings with departing friends become a ritual. Friends leave the dusty stream of people on the road to embrace one of the grownups standing in front of the house, then hurriedly return to their arduous journey ahead, where they hope to be safe from the approaching Russian army. Silently, I try to comprehend the meaning of the never-ending lines of humanity. Normally, when there is a lot of activity on the road, it means something exciting.

"Maybe a festival is coming to town," I think, but somehow I know that this is different. As I sit on the bench under the canopy of walnut trees observing the scene, the midday sun slowly turns to dusk. Suddenly I recognize a friend and jump up to run to her. We giggle at the layers of clothing my friend is wearing and at the small, neatly tied bundle slung across her shoulder. Joining hands, we skip along the road.

"Hildie. Get back here," Grandmother calls sternly. I pause. "Hurry up. Come back here at once."

I quickly run back to my grandmother, but am confused because she has never used such a tone of voice before.

"Let's go inside; it's getting dark and children need to be fed," says Grandmother as she scoops me into her arms.

Slowly our little family group walks along the veranda, being careful not to bump into each other in the darkness. Inside the courtyard, the pure flower-scented air is refreshing in the fading light. The multi-colored blooming flowers and delicate blossomed fruit trees are barely discernible. Little, garishly colored clay elves peep around fragrant flowering bushes. Grapevines creep on an elaborately carved trellis along the veranda, offering comforting shade and coolness on hot summer days.

This house is designed like most houses in town. Immediately inside the mammoth front door through which harvest-laden wagons enter, is a beautiful courtyard. The first room to the left of the veranda is the guest bedroom, which is always darkened to protect the luxurious velvet bedspread. A set of comb, brush, and mirror, all with an overlay of gold and silver inlay, is carefully set on snowy-white lace doilies. All is in waiting for the rare guest who is special enough to use this room — perhaps a visiting priest.

A spacious room next to the guest room is my grandparents' bedroom with adjoining double doors to the bedroom used by the grandchildren or less prominent guests. Following the veranda along the courtyard, next to the bedroom, is the kitchen used in the winter. Further along the veranda is the kitchen used in the hot summer.

Another set of gates, large enough for hay wagons to drive through, opens to the back yard were a huge manure pile in the middle of the yard is surrounded by stables for the cows and horses. Off to the side, a door opens to a smaller yard with sheds where chickens, pigs, and smaller animals are kept.

Opposite the back yard is the large room used as a summer kitchen and pantry. In the upstairs attic, grains, dried beans, and peas are stored for the long, cold winters. Next to the summer kitchen are steep stairs leading down to a cool, long, narrow cellar. On the earthen floor, wine barrels rest on wooden racks along both sides of the freshly whitewashed walls. Continuing on the ground level along the veranda to the back of the house is a huge barn where the wine press is stored in the winter months.

When the greenish-yellow grapes are sweetly ripe in the summer, the women gather them in the vineyards in huge baskets, which the men then hoist onto their shoulders and carry to the gigantic press in the barn. In the fall, young people enjoy each others' company in this barn while husking corn to be stored in huge bins. With much laughter and song, they tease each other, scarcely aware of the work being done by their industrious hands.

On this evening, Grandfather switches on the electric lights in the summer kitchen and the women busy themselves with dinner preparations. My grandparents anxiously whisper so I cannot hear them. Fear and confusion creep into my being. After our family eats the delicious hot dinner in an unusual silence, Theresa pours warm water from the kettle on the stove to give me a sponge bath.

My grandmother watches us while she washes the dinner dishes in hot soapy water. After my evening ablutions, I hug my grandmother around her waist, "Good night, *Grossmutter*."

She pats my head with her soapy hand. I sense that the sternness from earlier is gone as she bends down to embrace me, returning my kiss.

Next I run to my grandfather, "Good night, *Grossvater*." He pulls me onto his lap with his big calloused hands. He winks at me and smiles, "Good night, Hildie. Don't forget your prayers." The prickly stubbles on his cheeks and the tough, work-worn hands flood me with reassuring strength as we hug and kiss.

I slide off my grandfather's lap. Theresa carries me to the children's bedroom in the front of the house, squeezing and bouncing me as I giggle contentedly in her arms.

"Come on, Hildie, let's say our prayers." We both kneel on the floor, reverently gazing at the picture of a dark, long-haired man whose head is encircled with light. The forefinger on his left hand points to his white-clad chest on which appears a blood-red heart from which tiny flames leap up around a cross. With his soft, brown eyes and his right thumb, forefinger, and middle finger pulled upward, he seems to be beseeching me to listen.

"Tell me again who this man is," I ask.

"That's Jesus. He loves little children and answers their prayers. He is in Heaven where everything is lovely."

After our prayers are recited, Theresa swings me up on the bed, tucks the covers snugly around me, and sings a lullaby. The confusion of the day fades as I drift into sleep, soothed by the Theresa's song. My young cousin quietly turns off the light and softly closes the door behind her.

During the night, I awaken to a strange sound. Frightened, I whimper.

"Shhhh," cousin Nicky murmurs, sleepily.

Again, I whimper, "What's that sound?"

"You hear the people walking and the wagon wheels on the road," he mumbles.

I sleep fitfully in the darkness, hearing the sounds of shuffling feet and creaking wagon wheels, falling into blessed sleep, and waking again to the sounds.

The next day as soon as I am up, I run outside and watch the tired people still moving in an endless stream, mostly strangers now. My grandparents and two cousins are doing their chores, occasionally joining me in my vigil on the bench under the walnut trees in front of the house. Sometimes they hug me or smile at me, or whisper reassuring words. With the coming of dusk, I wearily return to the house, where a bright light illuminates the summer kitchen as we eat our dinner in strained silence again. That night too, sleep is elusive because the shuffling and creaking causes an uneasiness within me. All night the sounds of people moving continue.

As I awaken the following morning, I am aware that something has changed. The sun is shining brightly through the lace curtains near my bed. My cousins are already doing their chores; I must have slept late. With a start, I sit up in bed. The sounds are gone.

Quickly I put on the poppy-flowered sun dress my grandmother has laid out for me. Fumbling, I slip my feet into my sandals and run to the front door, quickly opening it. All is silent in the golden sunlight, the stillness unbroken. Standing in the middle of the dusty road, squinting from the shimmering light, I look down one side of the road, then the other, and see nothing.

I run across the road, along a fence made with mud and bricks, to a neighbor's house. The unlocked door is ajar, so I go inside. No one is home. All the beds are made, the dishes neatly stacked in the cupboards, six wooden chairs carefully positioned under the table. Searching each room, I call for my friends by name.

I run out of this house and dash to another and another and another, but always I am alone. With each step, clouds of dust rise and cling to my tiny sandaled feet.

"Where are the people?" I mutter to myself over and over. Finally, I shout, "Where are the people?" But no one answers. I am alone in these empty houses, the dusty road, and the bright yellow sunshine.

Hours later, barely able to lift my tired feet, I return home to my family. Someone washes my grimy, tear-stained face, hugging and rocking me. I close my eyes from exhaustion, sighing deeply.

Chapter Two

"*Do you mind if I sip coffee during our session today?" I ask the psychiatrist.*

"By all means, drink your coffee. Is the room temperature comfortable for you?"

"Yes, it's fine. Thank you for asking."

"Anything come up for you from our last visit?"

Looking over the rim of my multi-colored pansies coffee mug, "I remember mostly things about my young years before the war. Good feelings."

"Want to share them with me? Were you happy?"

"I was the youngest in our extended family of cousins. I felt loved and special. Perhaps I was pampered. I realize that I lived in my own world."

"What do you mean by that?"

"Because I felt safe and loved I could lose myself in nature. In watching birds in flight or stretching out on dewy grass breathing in the smell of the moist earth." Pause. "It was worrisome for my mother."

"In which way?"

Sipping my coffee leisurely, I remark, "You know our time today and the last few weeks has been relaxing. Talking with you is like talking to a friend."

He smiles.

"Oh, yes, my mother." I continue. "Well, I was a dreamer, which worried her because I wasn't all that interested in school and learning. She wasn't the most patient person. I remember one day,

she was helping me with school work at a round maple table by the window. She was pressuring me to pay attention, but I pointed out that the pattern in the lace curtains looked like a bird. I asked her if she saw it."

"What did she do?"

"I think for a moment she entered my world trying to see the curious wonder in the everyday mundane as I saw it. But then she just threw her hands in the air in defeat. I wish I could tell her how important those dreamy highly curious times have been for me throughout my life. And, that I have learned how to survive in a harsh world."

Staring off into space I am lost in my thoughts. I am startled to notice the length of time I have been in my thoughts.

"Everything about the war for me is tied to my mother," I comment. Taking in and letting out a barely audible breath, I say, "I wonder what kind of person I would be if the war had never happened."

~ ~ ~ ~ ~ ~

*W*ith looming clouds of impending military engagement in the Balkans, my grandparents in Miletitsch hurriedly make arrangements to send me home to the city of Zombor to be with my mother and sister. Although conflicting rumors of military move-ments cause uneasy feelings in the city, somehow my innocent world is still protected. The only entrance to the street where we live in Zombor is a large heavy door that is always closed, and often locked. I spend many happy hours lost in childish fantasies in the beautifully landscaped gardens amidst six garden apartments. I am happy to be home in our Zombor apartment with *Mutti* and Hedi.

One day, pedaling my much loved red tricycle as hard as I can across the smooth path, I close my eyes, feeling the delicious rush of wind lifting my golden braids against my face.

"I'm a bird. I'm a bird," I fantasize, "high in the sky close to the bright sun, above the green tree tops." Taking a quick peep to assure myself that I will not bump into a tree trunk, I again close my eyes tightly, leaning my little body forward, forcing my legs to pedal faster. Gazing at the golden sunlight, I gleefully laugh, "I can fly. I can fly." Slowly the wheels of my tricycle glide to a halt, but I continue to hold my smiling face toward the warm sun, still feeling the delicious rush of air on my skin. For a moment the radiant sun and I are one.

A sound interrupts my moment of oneness. Unable to identify the sound, I look around. All is unchanged. The leaves on the trees are still. The other children are playing tag in the huge fenced-in, verdant meadow next to the gardens. The tenants' carefully tended patches of lush vegetables are surrounded by a high wooden latticed fence.

I see my sister, Hedi, in her sturdy laced shoes chasing a boy, her golden braids flying behind her.

As they chase each other, they are careful not to fall into the deep trench a neighbor insisted on digging for safety in case of air attacks from airplanes. He is a serious young man who could not be deterred, despite the ridicule from other tenants. The children had watched him curiously as he shoveled the rich black earth over his head. Since the adults are in denial of any possible military danger in our city, they make fun of him, but he completed the trench. Now a ribbon of darkness stretches across the emerald green meadow.

The sound is louder. I glance at a white-haired grandmother sitting comfortably on a cushy chair in her garden, knitting pink baby booties.

"It sounds like thunder," I think. "Like rolling thunder." Looking up at the sky, I see that there are no dark stormy clouds. Now the sound frightens me because it hurts my ears and the ground is shaking. Sitting very still on my tricycle, straightening my spine, I search all around again. I see my mother pointing to the sky while talking to the young man who had dug the trench. The children stop playing, also staring at the sky. All activity stops as if frozen in a photograph.

Gazing upward, I see a tranquil, cobalt-blue sky and white fluffy clouds. To the left, clusters of tiny crosses swarm into a cloud. Now the sky is tranquil again, but the thunder and vibrations are increasing. Still peering at the sky, airplanes suddenly fly out of the clouds, becoming larger each second.

People start running and shouting. A man's strong arms whisk me off my feet. I scream as the sky and earth tumble upside down for me. Figures rush past me as I am carried and then roughly pushed down into the dark, damp trench.

Clawing at the black, clammy earth, I scream, *"Mutti! Mutti!"* I am unable to reach the top of the black slippery walls of earth, and bodies are squeezing me.

Suddenly my mother grabs me. "I'm here, Hildie. I'm here," as she pulls me tightly to her bosom in the utter confusion.

"Where is Hedi?" my mother shouts, attempting to stand up amid the tangled bodies. As quickly as the shadow of death appeared in the sky, it passes over the frightened people below. Fate has destined others for doom that day.

My mother and I find Hedi unharmed just as she is scrambles up from the damp trench and sprawls on the clean, green grass gasping for air. My mother looks for the young man who grabbed and shoved me into the trench, her dark brown eyes glinting with anger.

When she finds him she says, angrily, "Don't you ever touch either of my girls."

He is equally upset and shouts back, "How can you be so ungrateful? I was trying to protect her."

"If my children need protecting, I'll do it. You frightened Hildie unnecessarily. We were in no danger." Uneasily he notices my soiled khaki shorts and white blouse. My hands and face are covered with black earth. Lowering his eyes, he walks away muttering, "I only wanted to help."

I ask, "*Mutti*, why is everyone afraid of the airplanes? There were so many. Why were they so loud? My ears hurt when they flew above."

"The planes were filled with bombs. That's why they made such a deep rumbling sound and the earth shook."

"Bombs? What are bombs?"

"They drop them from the sky. When they hit the ground, they explode, hurting people."

"But how? If I run fast enough, they can't get me. I'll ride my tricycle. Are they going to drop the bomb here?"

"No. The airplanes are heading somewhere else. I don't know where."

"But..."

"I don't know any more. That's enough of your questions." She pauses. "Would you like to play in a tub of water in the yard?"

"Yes, *Mutti*, yes!" I answer excitedly. I love playing in the water by myself.

Lugging a large, white porcelain tub into the yard, my mother puts in a few buckets of cold water from the rain barrel. "Hildie, take off your clothes while I get hot water. Leave on your underpants."

When she returns with a steaming kettle, she pours the hot water into the tub, swishing it back and forth with her hand. "How's that, Hildie? Put your hand in the water to see if it's warm enough for you."

"It feels nice. Now can I get in? What if the water gets cold? I don't like it when the water gets cold. I get goose bumps." In my childish babble, I hardly notice my mother swinging me into the shallow, tepid tub of water.

"There now, how does that feel, my little fish?"

"Little fish," I repeat giggling.

My mother gently washes off the dirt from my face, arms, and legs. "Now you look like my little Hildie-bildilie again. All nice and clean."

Our eyes meet affectionately, smiling. My mother kisses the top of my golden head. "You may play with this bar of soap. Just call me if you need more warm water."

I imagine that the bar of soap is a little boat floating in the water. I slide it up the white enameled sides of the tub and around the rim. After a while, I shout, "*Mutti,* I need more warm water." No answer.

"*Mutti!*" I shout louder.

"All right, just a minute. Stop your shouting, you'll wake up the dead," my mother answers.

A few minutes later, my sister stomps down the sidewalk with the water kettle in her hand. "Here's your water, you little pest," she says, pouring the hot water down my back. Hearing my screams, our mother rushes toward us,

"Now what's going on? What happened to your back? Oh, Hedi, why did you do that?"

With her feet firmly planted on the ground, Hedi looks directly into *Mutti*'s eyes, "Well, she asked for warm water, and I gave it to her. She's such a crybaby," she says disgustedly.

We are too involved to hear the distant buzzing sound, but now we stop talking to see airplanes directly above us against a cloudless sky in the approaching dusk.

"Why are the planes back, *Mutti*?" I ask drawing closer to my mother.

"They're going home. The planes are empty now," she answers quietly. "Notice, we can hardly hear them and they are flying much higher now."

We watch the cluster of airplanes getting smaller and smaller, leaving only a faint buzzing sound as they disappear.

"Come, children. Let's go inside. I'll get supper ready while both of you wash up. Put on your pink flowered nightgowns, and unbraid and brush your hair. Remember to do a good job brushing your teeth."

After dinner, we kneel on the floor next to our bed, making the sign of the cross by lightly touching our foreheads, chests, and both shoulders. Together we recite the *Our Father,* asking for blessings for our family and all the people on the road. Our mother tucks us into bed. Switching the light off, she leaves the room. We fall asleep at once. It has been an unusual day.

~~~~~~~

*D*eep in the night, loud voices and crashing sounds awaken me. "*Mutti,*" I cry. "Where are you? What's going on?"

I see a flash of light outside the windows. Frightened, I jump out of bed in the darkness running on the cold tiled floor. Standing on the patio outside, my mother, sister, and other tenants are looking over the rooftops. The sky is completely illuminated in a steady blaze. Quickly I run to my mother to take her hand, asking, "*Mutti,* what's wrong? Why is it so bright over there? Is it a fire?"

"We don't know. It sounds like they're dropping bombs far away from here, but the constant glow in the sky doesn't make much sense," answers my mother.

The group stands in silence observing the illuminated sky. My mother takes Hedi's and my hands, whispering, "Let's go inside."

We walk through the dark rooms without switching on a light. *Mutti* slips us under the covers, saying, "Try to go to sleep. If you wake up and I'm not here, don't start crying. I'll be right outside the door with the other people. Don't make so much noise that they can hear you across the city. Did you hear me, Hildie?"

"Yes, *Mutti,*" I answer sheepishly. I sense Hedi shooting a hot glance in my direction and smirking in the darkness. "Can't we have a light on?" I ask.

"No," answers *Mutti.*

"But why not? Just a little light. You can stand it on the floor," I cajole.

"No. It's best not to attract attention should the airplanes fly overhead. Good night," she says sternly and leaves the room.

"Hedi?"

"No. You can't snuggle against me. Get your foot away from me; it's too close."

"Do you think the fire will get our house? Are you afraid?"

"Why should I be afraid? It isn't fire. Didn't you hear *Mutti*?" Before I can answer, she says, "I'm tired. Good night."

The outside light shines through our windows across the ceiling and bedroom walls creating oddly elongated shadowed shapes. Watching the shadows, I slowly I slide my leg under the cover until it rests on my sister's body. Comforted by her warmth, I fall asleep.

~~~~~~~

*T*he next morning and the following days are filled with confusion. The adults speak endlessly, with some arguing loudly, others walking around in a daze. Often, they cluster in groups speaking in hushed voices. Signs of the advancing chaos are becoming more visible. We sisters look to our mother, who continues her routine of caring for us. But she is distant, often reprimanding us harshly, her dark brown eyes troubled, deep furrows lining her face.

We learn that the bright lights in the evening sky were flares dropped by England to illuminate their bombing sites. The chaotic nightmare is getting closer. From a neighbor's large bay windows, my sister, mother, and I bear witness to yet another endless stream of people passing by, day and night, carrying their meager possessions.

While having lunch in our tiny kitchen, my mother says sternly, "Don't ever pick up anything from the street. Do you hear me?"

Startled, my sister and I stare at her. "Did you hear me—nothing, ever!"

Hedi says, "You mean because..."

"Yes," interrupts our mother.

I look at Hedi's face, then at *Mutti*'s and they both are looking at me. "I never go into the street. The horses are too scary. You told me never to cross the street," I say defensively.

"I mean, don't pick up anything from the sidewalk or street or garden or anything that does not belong to you," my mother says, exasperated.

"I never take anything that doesn't belong to me. Never."

Patiently my mother explains, "Someone is putting objects and toys around the city that can hurt people, especially children."

"What kind of toys? How can a toy hurt me?" I ask. My mother scrutinizes my trusting, innocent blue eyes. Taking a deep breath, she says, "This morning, a little girl picked up a fountain pen from the sidewalk. It exploded and hurt her."

"How can a fountain pen hurt you? Well, I'll never pick up a pen, I promise," I say.

"Don't pick up anything—next time, it might be something else."

"Why would anyone want to hurt children? Where was she hurt?"

"She's in the hospital. No more questions. Just do as I say. Understand?"

"Yes, *Mutti*," I answer. But I do not understand.

On this stormy, cold night, *Mutti* is deep in thought while cooking dinner. Often she interrupts her work to dash outside. Returning to the cozy, warm kitchen, she barely notices Hedi and me watching her distracted behavior.

Suddenly, from somewhere outside our apartment, we hear a raspy voice cry out, "Kathe, Kathe. Help me."

"*Mutti*, someone's still calling you," I say.

"I know, it's Liessi. She's very sick. She is leaving her home with her father and daughter."

"Kathe," calls the voice again.

Our mother abruptly leaves our apartment with a bowl of steaming hot chicken soup. We sisters continue eating our supper in silence. When she returns, *Mutti* stands by the moss-colored, ceramic-tiled stove, warming herself and drying her damp wool coat while running her fingers through her wet, dark chestnut hair. Rain drops pelt our windows.

"Is she any better?" asks Hedi.

"No. I can't find a doctor to take care of her, and the hospitals are filled."

"If she's sick, why not bring her in here where it's warm and dry?" says Hedi.

"I can't do that. Soon we may have to leave and you girls might catch what she has. I'm taking care of her. She is dry under the gangway, and I'm keeping her warm with hot water bottles."

"We promise not to get sick. Please bring her inside," we plead. "She's your friend."

"Kathe," the voice calls again.

Quickly our mother pulls on her damp, navy-blue wool coat.

"I can't!" she shouts, hurrying to the armoire where she pulls out a warm down comforter. Opening the kitchen door, she braces herself against the chilly rain and slashing wind outside.

All night long, the woman calls mournfully for "Kathe" to help her, and we girls plead with *Mutti* to let the woman rest in our apartment. Our mother ministers to her friend in the bitter cold throughout the night. In the morning, the ill woman and her family leave with their horse-drawn wagon.

~~~~~~~

When the sun appears later in the day, I pedal my red tricycle, retracing the clay-bricked path through the maze of gardens. I stop often, closing my eyes while breathing in the delicious, fresh fragrances of the rain-soaked earth and newly cleansed leaves of the shrubs and trees.

Standing very still, I look intently at the branches of a bush. My eyes follow the trail of a tiny, rainbow-hued droplet of water slowly rolling down the center spine of a leaf, dropping to the leaf below, and splashing on the reddish bricks in a burst of tiny sparkling bubbles of light. Moving closer, I see a necklace of prisms delicately dangling captured sunlight outlining each leaf. Lightly tapping the leaf, I am startled by the cold splash of water on my face. Smiling, I tug on more branches, enjoying the shower of prisms on my head.

"Good morning, *Frau* Weiler," says a deep male voice.

I recognize it as the voice of a tall, intense man who wears a well-tailored gray military uniform, hat, and highly polished black boots that reach to his knees. Another man in a similar gray uniform had spoken to the German tenants a number of times about leaving Hungary. One family has already left, and the others are making preparations to go. But my mother resists all efforts to encourage her to leave. Although she keeps it a secret from the German soldiers, my mother feels secure about our safety since the Russians and Americans are allies. Before her marriage, my mother, her sister Mary, and my grandfather had worked in the United States, and they are United States citizens.

Since the first soldier was unable to convince my mother of the need to leave the city, the German Commandant in charge of evacuating the city has had long, strained discussions with her, which always end with the soldier hurriedly striding out of the apartment. Our mother's face is pale and tense.

Quietly, I leave the safety of the warm, moist, filtered light to stand close to my mother while the two adults engage in terse conversation.

My mother glances down at me, saying, "What happened to your hair? It's all wet."

"The rain got it wet," I answer.

Distractedly, my mother lightly rumples my wet blonde hair. "It hasn't rained in hours," she says. The Commandant stops talking in mid-sentence, and glances down, too.

"The bushes rained on me," I explain.

My mother looks at me quizzically and then the two adults resume their conversation. Over and over he repeats, "You must leave. You must leave, I can't force you, but you must leave."

"No, I won't. I told you, no." My mother twirls around and enters our apartment, slamming the door. Another quick glance at me, and the Commandant leaves the yard with long, angry strides.

Standing alone now, I search for someone to talk with. Seeing *Fraulein* Schmidt sitting on the ground at the back of the yard, I skip toward her. "Hello, *Fraulein* Schmidt," I flash a smile at the old woman.

"Oh," greets the startled woman, squinting through her large bi-focaled eyes against the bright sunlight.

"Oh, Hildie, how are you?" *Fraulein* Schmidt's hands flit to her flushed cheeks, then her right hand flutters sideways, patting her neat, cottony white hair. Bending her head, she returns to sorting articles in the open suitcase on the ground.

Plopping myself opposite the frail woman, I ask, "What are you doing?"

"I'm going through all my things in the attic. I will be leaving tomorrow," she explains.

I pick up an embroidered cloth. "Who do these things belong to?" I ask, leaning closer to the suitcase looking for treasure.

"This belonged to my mother. Those are pillow covers she made for my hope chest," *Fraulein* Schmidt laughs nervously. "I didn't need them because I never married. I never found a man as wonderful as my father. My father gave this hair brush and mirror to my mother for Christmas."

My fingers trace the design of mother-of-pearl roses around the mirror and handle.

Wanting to escape from the older woman's unhappiness, I say, "I have to go. I hear my mother calling."

As I skip toward our front yard, I listen to the slapping, scraping sounds of my sandaled feet hitting the brick path. Hearing the heavy front gangway door slowly creak open, I skip to see who it is.

"Hi, Peter," I call. "Did you come to play with me?"

"No. Let's talk in the garden." As we walk, I gaze into Peter's dark brown eyes, which appear to be more solemn than usual. My playmate is always quieter than the other boys. Even when two classmates and I were rabbits in a play two weeks ago with Peter, he was often quietly observant, although I remember that he laughed when I twitched my nose, imitating a rabbit, and when I playfully pulled one of his large, white, furry rabbit ears. All four children laughed when we saw the others dressed in the white flannel costumes our mothers had made. We were covered from head to toe, with only our faces peering out. We hopped around noiselessly in our flannel-covered shoes and held our hands awkwardly in front of us, unable to pick up anything.

"Did your mother show you the pictures of us in our rabbit costumes?" I ask.

"Yes, it was all very silly."

Sitting down on the garden bench next to each other, I tease, "But you laughed. You know you liked being in the play and dressing like a bunny. Your left ear kept flopping over your eye." Despite himself, he smiles. We sit on the bench enjoying our shared moment of friendship.

"What's that in your hand?" I ask. Peter is clutching a small golden box.

Our eyes meet as pools of limpid dark brown gaze into the blueness of the clear sky.

Peter says, "We're leaving tomorrow and I want you to have this." He lays the box into my hands.

"Oh, Peter, it's beautiful. Thank you." I watch the sun's reflection dancing on the golden surface as I tilt the box in opposite directions.

"You know, that's gold on the outside," he says.

"Really?"

"When the war is over, we'll get married. Always keep this box and when I'm grown up, I'll buy you a beautiful gold watch that you can keep. It'll be my engagement present to you."

"We're going to get married and you'll buy me a gold watch?" I ask shyly.

Bending his head, he studies his black shoes, "Yes. Will you wait for me?"

"Yes, Peter, I will."

Awkwardly we stand up, looking deeply into each other's eyes. He turns and leaves.

During dinner that evening, I hold the box in one hand on the table, eating my vegetables with the other.

"What's in the box?" asks Hedi.

"Peter gave it to me. We're engaged."

"What?" asks *Mutti*. "When did this happen? How did you get engaged?"

"When the war is over and we're older, he's going to buy me a gold watch as an engagement present and put it in this box."

Hedi grabs the box and opens it, "It's empty. He didn't buy you a watch."

"I said he was going to and we're going to be married." *Mutti* leaves the table, busily moving pots on the stove.

"He's never going to buy you a gold watch," says Hedi.

"Yes, he is. He promised."

"No, he won't. He'll forget."

Suppressing a smile, *Mutti* rejoins us at the table. "Well, you never know what will happen. But a lot can happen between now and when you are grown up, and he may not remember to buy you a watch."

"Yes, he will! I know he will. That's why he gave me this golden box," I feel my face getting flushed.

"That's not gold, that's just a cardboard box covered with gold-colored paper. Are you stupid!" sneers Hedi.

"Hedi," *Mutti* intercedes, "now you have to admit that this is a very pretty gold-colored box Peter gave her."

"But..." starts Hedi.

"It is a pretty box, isn't it, Hedi?" our mother says sternly. I notice a flicker of a smile pass between Hedi and *Mutti*. Hedi stops mid-sentence.

"If you're done with your dinner, help me clear the table, Hildie. Hedi, get the enamel washbasin and put it on the table. I'm going to wash your hair tonight." She pauses. "Better take your golden box off the table and put it in a safe place," she says as she turns toward the stove.

~ ~ ~ ~ ~ ~

A few days later, I again hear the Commandant and my mother arguing back and forth. My mother heatedly makes the point that we will be safe if we stay. He shouts at her, "Woman, think of your children. Nothing will protect them when the Russians discover that their father is in the German army. They won't care if you are separated from your husband. You can't believe the terrible things that have been done to women and children by the Russian soldiers. Trust me, all the stories you have heard are true, but there is more, so much more that has not been heard yet. And if you think you are safe here, you are very much mistaken! The Serbians and Hungarians hate us Germans. You know that! And, once the German army is gone, there will be no one to protect you from the Russians."

Fear creeps into *Mutti*'s eyes. For a long time, she looks at Hedi and at me, as if letting the words she just heard echo in her brain.

"Pack now, this minute. Our convoy will be departing immediately after I leave you. I'll help you pack. I'll see that you and your daughters catch a train that will take you away from the Russian army," the soldier implores.

Lowering her eyes, *Mutti* agrees.

My sister and I follow the two adults racing toward the house. Quickly they pull suitcases from under the beds and throw clothes haphazardly into them.

"Girls, think of what we might need. We will be gone a long time. Think. No toys, no dolls, just what we need to survive," says

Mutti. I pack Peter's gold box in a suitcase, but when I am not looking, my mother slips it into a drawer.

Soon the frenzied packing is done and the large suitcases are snapped shut. While the Commandant carries them to the waiting truck, our mother packs small valises for each of us. Then, with one last look through every drawer, every room, our mother leaves the safety of our apartment.

"*Mutti*, wait. I have to get something," says Hedi. She sprints back inside, grabs a handful of our mother's beautiful, colorful needlepoint canvases of red poppies, peaceful pastoral scenes, brightly colored peacocks, bountiful bouquets of flowers, still life of baskets of fruit, and more. Running back to the waiting military vehicle, she tightly rolls the canvases into a compact package.

When *Mutti* sees what Hedi has in her hands, she says irritably, "Leave that here. We have no room. We can't carry them."

"We have room. Look, I rolled them up into a very small roll," says Hedi, who seldom cries, near tears.

"All right, stick it in my bag over here. Hurry, get in the truck. The soldiers are ready to leave," says *Mutti*. Swiftly Hedi stuffs our mementoes deep into the bottom of the bag, without realizing that they would be precious heirlooms of a way of life for future generations of our family.

The overhead canvas is rolled back on the gray truck parked on the street that is filled with soldiers wearing dreary gray uniforms and helmets strapped under their chins. Piling our luggage among their legs in the middle of two rows of wooden benches, they make room for us on the benches by squeezing closer together, being careful to keep their rifles ready between their legs. Speeding through the eerily empty city streets, the truck follows the jeep of the Commandant and his driver to join the convoy of retreating military and fleeing civilian refugees.

Part II

During the War
The Refugee Experience

Chapter Three

*T*oday I am fidgety in Dr. Gregg's office. Again it is a sweltering, humid Louisiana day. I am wearing a beige wide-brimmed hat and dark sunglasses in his office to protect my eyes from the glare. I squirm sideways slouching then straightening my spine on the brown leather chair. My hands grip the arms of the chair, then flutter helplessly into my lap. I cross my arms tightly over my chest. I feel jittery inside.

"Would it help if I closed the window blinds?" he asks.

"Maybe. I don't know. The sun is so much stronger here than in Chicago. I can't stand it." He closes all the blinds, and I slide my smoky gray lenses off my face. Absent mindedly I squish my hat behind my sandaled feet under the chair.

"What's wrong today?"

"I had another flashback just as I was turning into your driveway. I spilled my coffee all over my skirt. I almost turned around to go back home."

"But you decided to come."

"I don't know why I'm here. I should be at home. I'm not feeling well. I have a throbbing headache." With shaking hands I massage my temples. "This seems different from other times."

"How is it different this time?"

"I don't know. I can't calm down. I have to go. I can't be here today." I bolt out of my chair and start pacing back and forth inside the air conditioned room across from the glass French doors. With unseeing eyes, I walk a narrow path on the polished wood floor, back *and forth through the slivers of sunlight sliding from the windows into the darkened room.*

"Where are you?" he asks ever so gently.

"It's...the war...the war...everything is changing." Stuttering, I fall into my memory.

~ ~ ~ ~ ~ ~ ~

*W*e travel with the convoy of German soldiers as it moves from Zombor, Hungary toward Czechoslovakia. An eerie silence greets us as we drive through one deserted town after another. Scout troops sweep through each town to ensure that all German citizens who want to leave have been evacuated.

At night the soldiers bivouac us in empty houses and find food for us. Before dawn the convoy continues at full speed. A number of old people, women, and children are added to our little group as we speed to catch up with the last refugee train heading for Germany.

Although the soldiers must find retreating difficult, they sing beautifully poignant songs of strolling through green flower-strewn meadows, or climbing their beloved mountain peaks where the edelweiss bloom, or stalking deer in the early morning dew of the Black Forest in Bavaria. Their voices betray pent-up emotions when they sing of the intense bonds of friendship and the women who are waiting for them at home.

In Budapest, Hungary, we finally catch up with the train. Piecing together bits of information, we deduce that we are traveling to Vienna by way of Czechoslovakia. During those first few days on the convoy, the relentless pace of the soldiers is exhausting, but our lives have an orderly regularity each day. However, on the train we become part of utter confusion and chaos. No one seems to be in charge. Sometimes we are informed that we are heading toward a certain city, but upon arrival find that we are at a different location. Maps are unavailable. If a person has a map it is confiscated by train superintendents. All we know is that our final destination is Germany.

We live in constant fear of being on the wrong train heading toward the advancing Russian army. Or there is the fear of missing connections with a train. We never know if another train will arrive in one hour, a day, a week, or not at all. Nor do we know ahead of time where the train is going. Always in the back of our minds are nagging questions: What if the Russians are too close to us? What if the train does not come? What if the train comes, but does not stop to pick us up?

In desperation, some refugees sit on top of their possessions on the railroad tracks to keep the train from whizzing by without stopping to allow them to board. As soon as we pile our belongings between the tracks, my mother looks down one side and then the other. Then she decides it is too dangerous to huddle on the tracks, since there is no way of foreseeing if the speeding train will be able to stop in time to avoid hitting us. She instructs my sister and me to drag our baggage back to the train depot.

Many times we lug our meager possessions from one town to the next. Refugees are generally unwelcome because of the food shortage, but schools or huge halls are usually available for the homeless. There we can rest and receive some nourishment.

~ ~ ~ ~ ~ ~ ~ ~

"Hildie," calls Dr. Gregg from far away. I become aware of resting my head against the leather chair, my legs crossed at the ankles. "What is going on with you?"

"I don't know."

"Would it help if you lie down on the couch?"

My eyes swing around the room, past the bookcases stuffed with papers and books. I never noticed the couch in the corner next to the wall beneath a row of windows. "No...I don't think so...I don't know...I have to leave...I want to run," I stammer, haltingly tugging my blue-and-white striped, coffee-stained skirt over my knees.

"Why not try the couch? If you don't feel better, you don't have to stay on it. Just give it a try."

"Where will you be?"

"I'll be sitting on a chair right behind your head."

"You have used this couch before during therapy?" I ask.

"Not often, but sometimes it helps."

Gingerly, I sit on the edge of the flowered quilt on the couch. Swinging my legs up on the cheerful colors, I settle my head on the pillow. On the left, strands of sunlight shine through the closed blinds. Automatically I am drawn to the light. Dreamily my left hand glides through the brilliant light. In some unexplained way, the light calms my mind and heart. I become focused, "OK, let's start."

"Do you know what brought on the flashback?"

"No, I was just driving. I found the bright sun very irritating even with my sunglasses on. I don't know why, but I became very afraid and felt cold. I miss my mother so much. She died about 20 years ago – she was only 53 years old. And then, everything went blank for a few seconds. I think these episodes must be getting worse. I have never been shaken like this before."

"Do you have any thoughts on what this may be about?"

"Just something with Vienna. A train. My mother," I answered. I gasp.

"What is the matter?" he asks.

"I can't breathe." I can barely say the words. I am unable to move my face, my lips, my neck, my chest.

"Tell me what is happening."

He comes from behind my head leaning his ear near my mouth, "I can't breathe," I croak through clenched teeth. "Feels like a heavy weight is pressing down on me. Help me."

For a moment, he looks down at me. Hesitantly placing both his hands above my chest, he asks, "May I press down?"

A slight movement of my eyes gives him permission to proceed as I continue gasping for air. He places his hands ever so lightly on my chest. The pressure increases until suddenly I hear a loud sound like ice breaking in my chest. I can breathe again!

"Are you OK? Would you like a glass of water?"

"I'm OK. Yes, please, some water."

Sitting up on the couch, I sip water from a paper cup. "What was that about?" I ask him.

"I don't really know."

"Did you hear the sound of breaking glass or ice?"

"Yes, I did. I've never done that before. Are you in pain?"

"No pain. I feel lighter inside. The heavy weight on my chest is gone."

I am breathing normally now. "Thank you. What happened?" I ask again.

Shaking his head, he says, "I don't know what happened. I can't explain it." I return the empty paper cup to him.

"Are you able to continue? Do you want a blanket?"

Tightly wrapping the blanket around myself, I begin, "I remember this train journey in Vienna..."

~ ~ ~ ~ ~ ~ ~

On the train, I sit by the window wearily watching the outside world pass by. I am tired, and always hungry, but the view from the window periodically pulls my consciousness into green pastures where cows graze contentedly and red poppies dot expansive fields of yellow buttercups and blue cornflowers.

In contrast, near the cities I see bomb craters still smoldering, bombed-out buildings standing as symbols of the violence so recently visited upon them. When I see a young boy riding his tricycle I remember my carefree days in Zombor. My leg muscles tighten as I move my toes in rhythm with the boy's motions. My nose presses the windowpane, hoping to feel a breeze on my face. The window is my escape from a now incomprehensible and chaotic world. Each scene becomes embedded in my mind.

As soon as the brakes screech to a halt on the tracks, people start jumping off the train cars. Inside the train, people are putting on coats and pulling down suitcases from overhead compartments and dragging bulky packages from underneath the seats. Babies cry and people shout to each other over the din.

"Hildie! Hildie!" my mother calls as she shakes me. I turn my head, staring blankly. When I meet my mother's eyes, the boiling sea of human bodies and the loud noises cause me to sink back deep into the seat.

"Hurry!" says *Mutti*. "We're in Vienna. Maybe we can visit our cousins from Miletitsch who moved here. Hurry up. And don't look out that window again."

I barely get my arms into the sleeves of my coat before my mother yanks me out of my seat. She grabs Hedi's hand and we plow down the aisle through the crowded train.

On the platform, *Mutti* tells us, "Stay close to me. I have to get directions to Egert's apartment. But we have to hurry. We don't have much time. The train may be leaving within a few hours. Sir, are you from Vienna?" A man nods. "Would you be so kind as to tell me how to get to 12 Alserstrasse? Is it far from here? Can we walk it?" she shouts over the roar of the train engines.

"It's close to the train station. I'll tell you how to get there." My mother leans closer to the man's mouth and studies his moving lips to better understand his directions. Outside, she walks briskly, pulling me along. "*Mutti*, please stop. I'm tired."

"How can you be tired? You just sat on the train for days and nights doing nothing. We have to hurry. We don't want to miss the train. Hedi is able to keep up."

"We can catch the next train. Please, slow down," I beg, swallowing hard to keep from crying.

"Our cousins have a beautiful apartment and lots of food. You know Vienna is known for its fine pastries and beautiful music. Children, this is Vienna, home of Mozart, Goethe. We have to find our cousins," she says determinedly.

"But we may miss our train. They'll go on without us," says Hedi.

"We're going to see our cousins," my mother says, quickening her pace.

Looking down the sidewalk, I force myself to watch my feet as I place one foot in front of the other. I do not want to disappoint my mother, so I will my feet to move faster. "Pastries would be nice," I think.

After passing the same church twice, my mother asks for directions again. Finally we stop in front of an apartment building and trudge up three flights of stairs. The door flies open at the first knock.

"Kathe, it's you! We knew you were coming, but we didn't know when," says a smiling woman with chestnut-brown hair and eyes. The two women embrace tightly and kiss, tears filling their eyes as they stand in the doorway.

"Marianne, you look great. It's so good to see you."

"Oh, your *kinder*. Hedi, you're so tall. Look at you, Hildie, you're growing up, too," she says as she hugs the two of us. "Come in, come in; I'm not a very good cousin, am I, making you stand in this doorway?"

Stepping into the apartment, a man with red cheeks and sparkling blue eyes hugs our mother. "Kathe, oh Kathe, it's been so long. How are you?"

"I know, Hans. I know, a long time." Through their tears, the adults keep smiling and hugging one another. Three cousins from a little town called Miletitsch, reunited again in Vienna.

An old woman wearing a black vest and a floor-length gathered skirt covered with a black apron joins us. Her head is covered with a black babushka, just like the German farm women in Hungary wore.

"This is my *Mutter*, *Grossvater* Westermeyer's sister," says Marianne to Hedi and me. After the greetings, Marianne's mother hobbles to another room. "She injured her leg when she was a young girl," explains Marianne.

"Does it hurt?" I ask.

"No, not now; it's healed."

The three adults reminisce and swap stories, while enjoying the platters of food. Our cousin's hands gently caress the tops of our heads as she urges us to eat.

Startled by a strange sound coming from the cousins, I look at the adults, who look back at me. "Would you like another glass of milk, Hildie?"

"Yes, please." Sipping my milk, I hear the sound again. "What is that?" I demand anxiously.

"What, Hildie?"

"The sound you made. Is something wrong? Are the planes coming? What's wrong?"

Gently Hans takes my hands. "Child, we were just laughing. We're old friends. We were friends when we were as small as you and Hedi. Don't you remember what it feels like to laugh?"

"Laughing? Does that mean everything is all right?"

"Well, we're a little sad because you will have to leave soon, but now we're happy and laughing about things we did in Miletitsch. You remember Miletitsch, don't you?"

"Do you know *Grossvater* Westermeyer?" I ask eagerly.

"Yes, of course I do. Does he still have a booming voice that can be heard from one end of the town to the other?" We all laugh.

Five hours later, when Hedi, *Mutti*, and I return to the train, preparations are already underway to continue the journey. People jostle each other to get seats and store their luggage under their feet, where they can keep an eye on their belongings.

As *Mutti* lifts Hedi and me up the steep stairs to the car, she suddenly cries out, "Oh, no, I forgot my hat. Marianne gave me one of her hats and I left it on the table. Quickly, girls. Get up those stairs and sit down. I'll be right back."

"*Mutti*, no, you're not leaving me, are you?" I sob. "*Mutti*, don't go. The train will leave without you," I plead hysterically, running after her. Without turning around, my mother hops off the train and disappears into the crowd.

For an hour, I sit silently staring out of the window waiting for my mother to return. Then the train jerks, shuddering to life under my feet. In blind panic I kick and scream, "*Mutti! Mutti!*" as I fight the bodies in my way. A man's strong arms restrain me from jumping off the jerking train. Gripping me, he tries to calm me, but I keep twisting and turning in his arms, trying to free myself. All are silently watching me.

Some lean out of the window straining to see the last cars of the train. "There is your mother," a young male voice shouts. The train moves slowly.

"Let me go!" I scream. "*Mutti! Mutti!*" I bite and scratch the man holding me, straining against his arms. "Your mother is running. Two men are holding their arms out. She grabbed their arms and they're pulling her on. She's on," the young boy reports to the silent watchers.

Looking out the window beyond the people in front of me, I see the blur of the outside world pass by the speeding train. "*Mutti*," I whisper. My body becomes limp. I stop fighting. The man holding me brings his face close to mine, "Your mother is on the train," he says. "She can't walk through the cars, but when the train stops, she'll come back."

Searching the faces in front for my mother, I shake my head saying, "No, she isn't. I know she isn't." The man gently sits me on a seat by the window. Unseeing, I stare outside. In soothing voices, the women try to reassure me that my mother really is on the train, but I cannot respond. A hushed prattle begins among the group. Occasionally, someone looks at me and then helplessly turns away.

I sit rigid on the train bench, my thin shoulders and body slightly curled forward, my little legs hanging tensely over the edge of the wooden bench. My cheeks and lips set in deathlike stillness, all color drains from my features, a filmy glaze crosses my unseeing, unblinking, blue eyes.

I feel powerless, surrounded by invisible walls. No sound, no emotion, no sensation penetrates my soundless frozen world inside. An anguished voice within me repeats a prayer, "*Mutti, Mutti*, don't leave me, don't leave me. Please, please, don't leave me." I feel my life force mingle with the universal mists of life; slowly I succumb to the soft grayish mist, as delicate swirls sweep in me, through me.

My essence ebbs and flows with the mist, thinly spreading my identity to the vanishing point. The prayer fades, a sheet of ice replacing my emotions; I feel abandoned by my mother—a tiny black, insignificant lump left behind by my mother, my umbilical cord brutally severed.

Then, from within the core of my essence, there is a knowing that reverberates, "I will not give up." Louder, "I will not give up." A tiny prism of light wells up within me. As the quivering, shimmering rainbow prism expands, the frozen void is transformed into a brilliant, radiant, blinding white light.

Staring out of the window, I am aware of the bright midday sun fading into the late afternoon and the leaden sky of the dying day heralding dusk. Momentarily the train halts in the starlit night, waiting for another train to pass before proceeding. This short delay allows my mother time to return.

"Look, here is your mother," says the man who had restrained me earlier. My mother looks at my still body and my frozen features. She tries to hug me, but I push her away, choosing to remain behind the invisible walls where my emotions are in a sheet of ice.

Shocked by my unresponsiveness, she coos, "Hildie, it's *Mutti*. I'm here. I'm here. I'm safe." I let my mother hold me. "Hildie-bildilie, my little fish." These familiar words of endearment touch the icy sheet and slowly, I break through the invisible walls, through the frozen void. Some of my emotions return, and I am able to feel again. I start to cry while my mother rocks me.

Relieved to see me crying, the people return to the drama of their own survival. The man who had restrained me says to my mother, "You're lucky. You almost missed the train. We didn't think you were going to make it. None of us did—it was like a miracle. What were you doing?"

"My friend was holding something for me."

"What?"

She answers, "A hat."

"A hat? The hat you have on? For this you hurt your child?" This new information is repeated from person to person.

"I didn't think the train was going to leave so soon. Anyway, I got on, didn't I?" she adds.

Others join in a heated exchange, berating my mother for her irresponsible actions, but when the people see my frightened eyes, they stop their accusations and turn away.

Chapter Four

"*How was your week?" asks Dr. Gregg.*

"Not good. I slept for three days after I left here. It took all I had in the evenings to shower, dress, and go out for dinner with my husband. And then I would go back to bed when we came home." Sighing, I close my eyes resting my head on the back of the chair.

"Were you afraid at any time?"

"I don't know. The fatigue washed out all emotions."

"What else did you do this week?"

"I met with the Dean of the English department at LSU. Since the job market is dismal in Shreveport, I might as well finish my graduate degree."

"Do you think that it might be wise to wait a bit before starting your graduate studies?"

"I don't even know if I'll be accepted. I'll just fill out the application and see what happens. I took my GRE exam in Chicago." Pause. "I can't just let time slip by doing nothing productive."

"How will you manage your low energy issue?"

"Just like always – through sheer will power. I'm used to pushing myself toward a goal. I really want a master's degree."

"Why now?"

"I come from a family that values education. Unfortunately there never was enough money. I earned my undergraduate degree when I was 42 years old. It took me ten years because I was raising my little boy and girl. I was a stay-at-home mom for 15 years and took one

class at time. Now it's my time. I will have the luxury of going to school full time – it will be my only focus. This makes me happy."

"Any flashbacks this past week?"

"I'm really too tired to know if I'm in a flashback or just reliving my session from here with you. I'm somewhere – I don't know where."

~ ~ ~ ~ ~ ~

*T*he train, crowded with cold, hungry, tired refugees finally reaches a German town in the middle of the night. A large, chilly room with fresh straw strewn in the corners awaits us.

To the man in charge, my mother says in a loud, indignant voice, "Where do you expect us to sleep?"

"Anywhere you like," he answers curtly as his bulky gloved hands tightly tug his long woolen muffler around his neck. Wispy puffs of frigid air float between them as they speak.

"What? You expect us to sleep on the straw like animals? This room is ice cold. How dare you treat us so inhumanely?" My mother straightens herself to her full imposing height.

Too tired to care, I throw myself on the straw, wearing my maroon woolen coat, leggings, and hat. "Get up, Hildie. You're not an animal," *Mutti* reprimands.

"I doubt if you're used to better where you come from," scowls the man.

With great effort, my mother controls her anger by slowly enunciating each word, "We're Germans, well-educated and prosperous. We left everything, do you hear? Everything! If the Russians come here, you will lose everything also. The father of my children is fighting in the German army. Get us beds and blankets, and bring us some hot food." The man hesitates. "Now, this instant! These are German children and they will not sleep on straw like animals!"

A quick glance at the fox collars on our high-quality woolen coats puts him into action. "I'll see what I can do," he mumbles and scurries out of the building into the howling wind.

Large kettles of steaming coffee, milk for the children, and crusts of bread, as well as blankets, are distributed. In a few minutes, the children huddle to warm themselves around a blazing fire in the black, cast-iron stove. One by one, the children slip under the blankets on the straw. Because my mother refuses to let her daughters sleep on the straw, Hedi and I tiredly sit on the bare floor near the stove.

"Where are the beds?" asks my mother impatiently. "We are not animals."

The man in charge pleads, "Look, the room is getting warmer. We've given you hot food and warm blankets. We're poor farmers. We can't get you beds. This is all we can do."

Another refugee pats my mother's arm, "Let it go, Kathe. This is all we're going to get. Don't waste your energy. Thanks to you, we've been fed and are warm. Let's go to sleep. Daylight will be here soon."

"I guess you're right," she answers. To the man in charge, she snaps, "What are we having for breakfast?" He rolls his eyes to the ceiling. Glaring at him, she says, "Well, you better make arrangements right now." He hurries out of the room, slamming the door behind him.

"It's okay. Hildie and I don't mind the straw," says Hedi quietly.

Arranging the blankets for us, our mother mutters, "How dare they treat us like this? I'm sure when we get deeper into Germany, we will be treated well. These people are just ignorant."

We stay at this location for a few days while we wait for another train. My mother continues to harangue the townspeople, and they are glad to see the last of her when the train finally arrives.

~ ~ ~ ~ ~ ~

O n the train, days slip into nights and nights into days before we stop in a farming community. All around us is food, but most farmers refuse to share it with the refugees. My mother is forced to beg for food, walking from one farm to the next. One day, she sees a farmer walking toward his stable.

"Sir, do you have any food I can buy?" she asks courteously.

"No. I have no food for gypsies like you," he says as he curls his lower lip in disgust.

"We're not gypsies, we're German. My husband is in the German army. I need food for my children," she explains politely.

"If you're not gypsies, why are you here?"

"The Russians are coming. We had to leave our homes, everything."

"Well, you're stupid to leave. Even if the Russians do come, I'm not going to leave. This land has belonged to our family for generations," he says proudly over his shoulder while walking to a dilapidated lean-to shed filled with heaps of potatoes.

"Let me buy some potatoes from you. We are desperate."

He throws the bucket filled with potatoes to the pigs, "No. My pigs need to be fed."

"How can you be so cruel? We're human beings and you give the food to the pigs. When the Russians come, you'll lose everything."

"Never. Get out of here, and don't ever bother coming back, you and your gypsy children. You're all too lazy to work; that's your problem."

We three walk down the road to the next farm. "Do you have any work for me in exchange for food?" my mother asks a ruddy-faced farm woman.

"No," is the reply.

"Please. I'll do anything. My children need food," my mother implores.

"Are you gypsies?"

"No, we're German, my husband is in the German army."

"You don't sound German. Where are you from?"

"Hungary, but we're German." Although we speak German, it is a unique dialect developed over the past two hundred years of living in the Balkans.

"Too bad you didn't have enough sense to earn a living."

With great effort, my mother holds back her retort. My mother's parents have a more prosperous farm, larger and better managed than any she has seen in Germany so far. Humiliation stings her, but she is desperate.

"You do have a very nice farm. You have a right to be proud. Do you have any work for me? Anything!" begs my mother.

Looking piteously at us sisters, the woman's face softens. "You can pick apples in the orchard. Come, I'll teach you how to do it." She takes a big bucket and walks ahead in knee-high, manure-encrusted rubber boots. Quickly we follow her. In the orchard, branches of bountiful apples are propped up with wooden slats.

The farmer's wife instructs us, "Pick only the apples on the trees and put them into the bucket. Then when the bucket is full, bring it into that shed with the other apples. Here, let me show you. Take the apples carefully off the tree and carefully place them in the bucket. Be sure not to bruise them or they'll rot like those on the ground. We love eating apples in the winter." She looks at us sisters. "Don't eat any apples off the trees, but you can have as many you want that are on the ground. None off the trees, understand?" We nod in agreement, but look with dismay at the half rotten apples on the ground.

"What do you do with the apples on the ground?" asks my mother.

"We feed them to the pigs. They love apples."

When the farmer's wife leaves, my mother picks two of the ripest, juiciest apples off the tree and gives them to Hedi and me.

"But, she said we should only eat those off the ground," I protest.

"The apples on the ground are for the pigs. You are not pigs. You eat as many apples as you want off the trees. You are young ladies."

"The woman will be angry," I say, worried.

"She won't know. It'll be our secret."

"If she asks, I can't lie. You told me never to lie. And isn't it stealing to eat apples off the trees if she said not to?"

"No, it isn't stealing. You are a human being, not an animal, and humans eat the apples off the trees. The woman is ignorant, but we have to be very nice to her. Thank her every chance you get, and be mannerly. Maybe she'll hire me for more work in exchange for food."

"You're sure it isn't stealing?"

"Yes, I'm sure. Now sit next to Hedi and eat." In ecstasy, Hedi and I savor the sweet, red apples as the delicious juice dribbles down our chins.

It is like a holiday for my sister and me. While our mother picks apples, we play among the trees. Picking lemon‑yellow dandelions, we make necklaces for ourselves and a crown for our mother's soft curly chestnut hair. Hedi and I giggle. We sing songs and dance, holding hands in the glorious sunshine. A familiar rumbling shakes the earth. Standing perfectly still, we watch the airplanes overhead. Fortunately, we have not been in an air raid attack since Vienna, but watch daily as the loaded planes fly overhead, and then return without their deadly cargo.

When the farm woman returns, she smiles in amusement at our bright yellow necklaces, "My children used to love making necklaces like that when they were young. Of course, now they are all grown." She pauses smiling. "Well, how did you like the apples, girls?"

"They were very good," answers Hedi immediately. I remain quiet, smiling sweetly.

"Thank you," we say smiling. We both curtsy, bending our knees low.

"Did you eat the apples off the trees or the ground?" she asks me. Confused by the truth and the lesson on survival from my mother I stammer, "Thhhh, thhhh..."

"The ground, naturally," says my mother smoothly. "I hope you'll have enough left for the pigs. The girls were so hungry. We are so grateful for your kindness."

"Come back again tomorrow."

"Thank you. Could you possibly give my daughters some cheese or meat or milk?"

"I guess so," the farm woman replies reluctantly.

The next few days, we return to the farm, always being gracious and cheerful to our benefactress. Sometimes we sisters work with our mother. The old woman feeds us fairly well, but she begrudges us the food and seems glad when our little family leaves on the next train.

~ ~ ~ ~ ~ ~

*D*eeper in Germany, a refugee camp is set up in a huge castle that is within walking distance of a town. Rough wooden planks are hastily nailed into three-tiered beds. Without a physician or medicine, the camp attendants tend to the various illnesses as best they can. They consistently work to rid the camp of head lice and body fleas. Each individual receives a black, fine-toothed comb with instructions to run the comb through the hair, starting close to the scalp. At any sign of lice, the infected individual is given a special bar of soap for a vigorous washing. I hate the fine-toothed comb because it pulls my long hair when my mother combs it. No matter how much I try to avoid it, my mother never lets a day go by without a careful combing.

Despite their diligence, the attendants are unable to rid the camp of fleas and lice. They scrub floors and harass the refugees about daily combings and body hygiene, but nothing seems to stop the contagion.

There is an old man who sits by the window all day in his many-layered clothing covered by a dark overcoat and brown fur hat, which he never removes, even while sleeping. His long, greasy, gray beard covers his face and flows down his chest. His feeble eyes look out the window in an unseeing gaze. When he is not sitting on the chair by the window, he lies in bed. He is a cantankerous old man who lets no one near him. Nor does he talk with anyone, and he refuses to change clothes, bathe, or comb his unkempt beard. One day, two men drag the man screaming to the bathing room, where the attendants shave off his beard as the lice parade up their arms. All his clothes are doused with kerosene and burnt because the seams are also infested. After stripping his foul-smelling sheets, blankets, and pillows, these are all added to the orange flames of the bonfire. Sliding a knitting needle between the wooden bed planks, the orderly finds it covered with lice. Quickly, they drag the bed outside, adding it to the consuming flames. The old man's disposition worsens, but he never again hesitates to take a bath or change his clothes when the attendants remind him.

Among the refugees, there are heated debates about the treatment of the old man. All agree that old people should be treated with respect. Some feel that the attendants showed a lack of respect by forcibly shaving and washing him. Others argue that the attendants had acted wisely, since the flea and lice infestation could not be controlled because he had refused to cooperate. Shortly thereafter, the latter contention proves to be accurate because there are fewer vermin outbreaks, and those that do arise are easily treated.

Food is scarce. There are many days when my family has just one boiled potato to share among the three of us. I often cry because my stomach aches from hunger. One night, I cry continuously beseeching my mother, "Please, give me something to eat. I'm so hungry."

Unable to bear it any longer, my mother tells Hedi, "Take care of Hildie, I'll be back."

"Where are you going?" asks Hedi, raising her voice over my whining.

"I'm going out to get some food," my mother answers as she tightens the shiny black buttons of her coat and snugly twines a scarf around her head and neck.

"It's midnight. It's too dark. Don't go."

"I have to. Take care of her," my mother says as she strides out of the room.

"Oh, shut up, Hildie. Just shut up," Hedi commands, shaking me by the shoulders.

I whine more loudly, "Leave me alone. I'm hungry. My stomach hurts. Why can't I have something to eat?"

"Because there isn't any food, that's why. Shut up," she growls.

"*Mutti!*"

"She isn't here. She went outside to get you food. Just hope she doesn't get shot."

"Shot??"

"Yes, shot. Any civilian out after dark gets shot, and especially if she's caught stealing food. And it'll be all your fault."

"I don't want her to steal food."

"How else do you think she gets it? The camp food won't keep us alive. *Mutti* and I are hungry, too, but you don't hear us complaining. What do you think will happen to us if she doesn't return?"

"You think she may not come back?"

"Could be."

In terrified silence, I sit on my bed biting my nails, part of me slipping into the frozen void I experienced in Vienna. My sister sits next to me, waiting like a frozen statue.

It seems like forever, but finally *Mutti* returns. Triumphantly, she gives us her prize. I examine the strange root. "What is it?"

"It's cabbage root. I was lucky. The farmers cut off the cabbage heads and left part of the root. It was so dark I could barely see. I stumbled over the clods of earth and when I fell, I found these few roots," she says. "Maybe God was helping me."

"I don't like cabbage," I whine. "You know I have never liked cabbage. Don't you have some bread?"

Exasperated, my mother throws her hands in the air. "No, I have no other food for you. Eat what you have. You'll feel better. It will fill your stomach."

I see the pain in my mother's eyes and feel my sister's leg sharply kick my back. "Thank you. Please don't go out at night again. I'll try not to cry so much." Taking a bite of the root, I gag, wanting to spit it out, but because my mother is watching me, I swallow. Since my mother's eyes never leave my face, I am forced to eat the entire root. Hedi greedily stuffs her portion into her mouth, making her cheeks puff out like a chipmunk. It has been a long time since we slept without hunger pangs. On this night, we rest well with full stomachs.

~ ~ ~ ~ ~ ~ ~

"The potato truck is coming!" shouts one of Hedi's friends the next morning. Hedi dashes outside to join a group of twenty or so children whose ages range from five to fourteen.

"Go on, Hildie, see if you can get yourself a potato," says my mother.

"I don't want go."

"Go!" she orders.

Against my will, I walk down to the delivery ramp where the truck driver dumps heaps of potatoes colored the autumn brown of oak leaves and smelling of damp, moist soil. The children snatch one and run, while the guard chases another. "Hildie, grab one or two and run," encourages my sister.

I stand shyly looking at the potatoes and at the guard. Proud of their pilfering, the children leave one by one, until only the guard and I are left. "May I please have two potatoes?" I ask the guard courteously.

Pulling his forest-green felt hat down to his brow, he glares at me. "No."

I shrink back. A few days, later a truckload of golden apples is delivered, and my mother again insists that I get myself an apple. Again, I stand shyly by the glowing heap, watching the other children and the guard, but I cannot force myself to take an apple. Some children encourage me to take one fast and run anywhere; others make fun of my timidity. The guard watches me as I walk toward the castle, empty handed as usual.

This routine is repeated several times. My mother continues to insist that I join the other children when the delivery man comes. Her disappointment in my not learning how to take care of myself is hard for me to bear. I would gladly have done anything to avoid these unpleasant experiences.

One day, as usual, the delivery of potatoes arrives and my mother insists that I get myself a least one tiny one. As usual, I stand back, watching the children while they grab one or two earth-covered potatoes. Occasionally, the guard catches a child and with his soiled, stiff, leather gloves, cuffs him or her. Red-faced, he bellows at them, "Get away, you ruffians!" As is my practice by now, I am ready to return home empty handed, when the guard smiles at me and motions toward the pile of potatoes.

"Take one," he says.

Disbelieving, I point to my chest with my forefinger asking, "Me?"

"Yes, you."

I pick the biggest potato I can find and warmly say, "Thank you." Clutching my prize in both hands, I run to show my mother, who is overjoyed at my budding survival skill.

"Look, look, look, I have a potato and it's a big one."

"Now was that so hard?"

"No, the guard said I could have it."

"The guard said you could have it?" repeats my mother in disbelief.

"Yes, isn't it wonderful!"

"Mr. Grouch himself said you could have it? Are you sure?"

"Yes, yes. He said, 'Take one'." Bouncing up and down, I clap my small hands with joy. "And he shouted at all the kids, but to me, he spoke very nicely. He must like me. Do you think he likes me?"

"Yes, I would say he likes you. Did he smile at you?"

"Yes."

"I'll bet his faced cracked. Nobody's ever seen that man smile."

"You know, the kids are so mean to him. It's his job to save the potatoes for everybody in camp and if he didn't guard them, the kids would steal them all. He is a human being, you know."

"Yes, I guess you're right."

My routine continues as before. Sometimes the guard smiles and nods for me to take an apple or potato. Sometimes he just looks through me as if I do not exist and I leave empty handed. I dislike how I feel when he ignores me, but I am always quietly polite. I know that he is doing a hard job as well as he can. Our unspoken arrangement works well for both of us for the remainder of my stay at this camp.

~ ~ ~ ~ ~ ~

*A*lthough illness, disease, and death are an integral part of camp life, their existence has little meaning to me until an infant becomes ill.

Across the aisle from my bunk, a young woman and her infant share a bed near the floor. Often, I lie on my stomach in my upper bunk, rest my head against a rolled-up, itchy, pewter-colored blanket, and watch the young woman tend her baby. The baby frets and cries day and night despite the mother's constant care. Sometimes, she rocks the baby sitting in a semi-awake state. At night, she walks the narrow spaces between the beds, trying to keep the infant quiet. The infant rests on the mother's shoulder. A soft blanket covers the baby's head and trails down to the young mother's waist.

"*Mutti,* do all babies cry so much?" I ask after the baby has caused another sleepless night. "Did I cry that much when I was a baby?"

My mother smiles sadly. "You cried as all babies do, but not as much as this one."

An attendant looks in the room, and the young mother with the infant cradled in her arms asks anxiously, "Do you have some milk today? I only had a little yesterday, and you promised I would get some fresh milk today."

"Yes, you'll get some later. We're sending someone to another farmer after he's done milking his cows."

"But she's hungry now. She was hungry all night." The young mother swallows hard. "She won't stop crying. I don't know what else to do."

"Here, give me the baby. I'll hold her for a while. Why don't you rest?" the attendant coaxes. The mother pulls back and shakes her head. Gently, the attendant touches the young woman's shoulder, "You're tired. Let me walk her. I'll take her down to the kitchen. Maybe I can find some sugar for her. I'll take good care of her." Hesitantly, the mother releases her infant into the other woman's arms. After they leave the mother drops her exhausted body on the bed.

I open my mouth to ask my mother another question, but my mother places her forefinger on my lips. "Shhh, be quiet," she whispers. "Go outside quietly and let the poor woman rest. Her baby's very sick."

I tiptoe silently out of the room, but outside, I sit on the floor near the door waiting for the baby to return. Hours later the attendant brings the baby back and I follow her back into the room. The young mother's face glistens with newly shed tears as she stands by the window, gazing at the gray drizzle on the slabs of pavement outside. "How is my baby?" she asks anxiously.

"We gave her some chamomile tea with sugar. That seemed to calm her." The attendant gently removes the baby's soft beige blanket, exposing large boils on the infant's thighs, hips, and upper arms. "I washed her with chamomile tea, which seemed to soothe her, but we don't have very much left."

The adults are so absorbed in their conversation that they do not see me edge closer to peer at the infant's body. The attendant says, "She has another boil here. You aren't squeezing the pus out, are you?" The young mother is silent, her eyes fastening to the half-opened, yellowish, and feverish eyes of her infant.

The attendant swaddles the blanket around the infant before returning her to the mother's outstretched arms, "Don't squeeze them. It isn't good for her. Let me know when you need warm water. Here, give her this if she frets too much," she says as she puts a white cloth into the young woman's hand before leaving.

I stand near the young mother's knee, examining the infant's pale face. "Will that make your baby well? Did the doctor give her medicine?"

"Hildie, leave them alone. Come over here," *Mutti* calls sharply.

In a hushed tone, I assure my mother, "The baby will be better now. She got some medicine."

Putting her arms around me my mother says, "No, that isn't medicine. That's a pacifier made of cloth and sugar. We have no medicine."

"Well, the chamomile tea made the baby feel better. She'll get well now if the mother takes good care of her."

"There isn't much the mother can do and the tea can't help much."

"Oh, yes, it can too help," I insist determinedly. "The tea will make the baby well. I know it will. Can't we help?"

My mother shakes her head, "The only way we can help is to let them have peace. Don't talk to her and stop asking her questions. The baby's very, very sick."

My mother quietly leaves the room, but I remain. My eyes never leave the baby as I hold on to the conviction that there will be a complete recovery. When the young woman removes the baby's clothes to squeeze yellowish, whitish-green, putrid matter out of a boil on her baby's thigh, I caution her, "Don't do that. You're not supposed to do that." The young mother does not look at me, but she stops squeezing the boils and wipes the sickening waste off the baby.

"Here is a nice bottle of warm milk. See if she can keep it down," says the attendant as she enters the room. Eagerly, the young mother places the nipple into the infant's mouth, but the baby feebly sucks only once or twice, then stops. The mother pulls her baby closer to her face. "Drink, you have to drink," she cries anxiously.

"Let her rest. Don't force the milk on her. Maybe in a little while, she'll take it," says the attendant gently.

"The boils on her little arms are so big, and she's getting another one in her armpit." The mother's red-rimmed eyes plead for help.

The attendant sighs, "Don't squeeze them. I'll be back later." As she turns to leave the large room, I start to tell her that the young mother squeezed the boils again, but remembering my own mother's admonition, I remain silent.

My mother brings me a boiled potato and a glass of milk because I refused to leave my vigil near the ceiling. Sitting on top of my bunk bed eating absent-mindedly I am totally absorbed with the infant and young mother.

"Hildie, get down here and wash up for bed," says *Mutti*. After slipping on my nightgown, she carefully combs my hair with the hated fine-toothed comb, but my eyes are on the infant. The large room drops into an unearthly silence as one by one, the other children and adults creep quietly into their beds.

The baby retches and vomits. After an older woman gently bathes the infant, she securely pins on a clean diaper. She dresses the baby in a newly washed, snug, little knitted yellow and green hat and jump suit, and returns the tiny bundle to the young mother's waiting hands.

Hedi and I kiss and hug *Mutti* good night. "Say your prayers," she whispers to us.

I doze at the foot of my bed under the military blanket, resting my head on my arm. Sometimes I awaken to watch the shadowy figure below, pacing back and forth in the dimly lit room. Once the young mother stands at the foot of my bed near the aisle. Our eyes meet for a long moment. The mother lovingly pats her baby nestling on her shoulder under the soft blanket. All alone, she resumes walking her lonely celestial passage into the ether carrying the precious fading light of her flesh.

Deep in the night, I awaken. In front of the huge window, I see the silhouetted forms of the mother and infant in rays of luminous silvery light streaming from the blackness outside.

The next morning, a hushed, urgent voice awakens me, the sun blinding me as I focus on the room below. The attendant is bending over the young mother speaking so softly that I cannot quite understand. Shaking her head, the attendant leaves the young mother, who is sitting on the chair with unseeing eyes staring into nothingness. Now I see the infant's white waxen face.

The young mother changes her infant's diaper, crooning a quiet lullaby and murmuring affectionately. I see that the motionless infant is strangely quiet.

My mother motions me to come down from my bunk bed. Everyone else has already left the room. I enjoy the rare treat of being carried out of the room in my mother's arms. I long for the times in Miletitsch and Zombor, when a member of the family often held or carried me. I am comforted by a fleeting moment of closeness with my mother. She rarely carries me now.

Later in the day, when I return to the room with my mother, my eyes are riveted to that part of the room usually occupied by the infant. But the hollow-eyed young woman lies alone on her bed with vacant eyes. Her pale face is almost the color of her infant's earlier that morning.

"*Mutti*, where's the baby?" I ask.

"She died. She'll be buried later today or tomorrow."

"She can't be dead. The chamomile tea was helping her. The attendant will bring her back. She just took the baby for a walk, right, *Mutti*? She'll be back, won't she?" I plead. My mother shakes her head.

Outraged, I shout angrily, "It's her fault," pointing to the young mother. "She didn't take good care of her baby."

An attendant rushes in."What's all this commotion?"

I run to the young woman on the bed, hysterically screaming, "It's your fault the baby died. They told you not to squeeze her sores, but you did. I saw you." The young woman turns her face aside with a strangled sob.

My mother pulls me away from the bed. "What's the matter with you? She loved her baby and took good care of her."

"No, she didn't. She squeezed and all the ugly, greenish pus came out. They told her not to do that."

The attendant standing over me says, "I'm not a doctor. We have no doctors, no medicine, and very little food. I told her not to squeeze the boils so the baby could die in peace. I hoped that the mother would begin to let go of the baby just a little. She was a good mother."

My mother holds me close to her chest as I sob hysterically."You would have saved the baby, *Mutti*. I know you would have. You're strong. You got me the cabbage roots. You would have saved me, wouldn't you?"

"The baby was very weak and sickly. No one could have saved her. If you get sick, I'll take good care of you, I promise." But I know that death lurks everywhere all around us. My mother rocks me into exhausted sleep.

Burial services are held next day, but I stay in bed, watching the feathery snowflakes drift by the window. Two women support the sobbing mother when they return. Delicate, white snowflakes fleck their covered heads and coats. Wrapping a rough, leaden-gray blanket around the young mother, they help her sit on a wooden chair.

"My baby, my baby," moans the grief-stricken young mother. "If only I could have saved her. My husband never saw her. What did I do wrong with her? Why didn't God help her?"

"Maybe He did. Where she is there is no more pain, only joy. You took good care of her. All of us said what a wonderful mother you were. You had so much love and patience day after day, and nights you walked her so we could sleep. Your husband would be proud of you," says one of the women.

While they comfort the bereaved mother, no one notices me standing near the young mother's knees. Because of my confusion, I am unable to speak. I still have a little resentment toward the mother for squeezing the boils, but I miss the baby too, and I share the mother's loss. In her grief, the young woman strokes my blonde hair.

"I'm so sorry," I mumble.

"So am I," is the reply.

As the days pass, the young woman, pale and wan, rarely speaks, and walks as if she carried a great burden on her back. Sometimes she gets up at night and stands by the window softly crying. Living seems to be a great effort for her.

~ ~ ~ ~ ~ ~

*R*eports of the Russians' approach filter through the camp. "I wonder how that pig farmer feels now that the Russians are on his land," I hear my mother saying. "I wonder if he wishes now that he had given us some food. Of course, he may be dead if he didn't leave. Well, everything works out for the best in the end. He was a stubborn man. His land meant more to him than his life or the lives of his family. If he left despite what he said, now he is a refugee too and knows what it means to be hungry and cold."

Looking at Hedi and me, she says, "Soon we'll have to leave. I've been told by the transport director."

"Where are we going?" Hedi asks.

"No one knows. We have to do as we are told. I hope that we will be safe there," my mother answers.

"When?" asks Hedi.

"In a few days, after Christmas. You know, tonight is Christmas Eve. I have no presents for you girls. I'm really sorry."

"Will we get some candy?" I ask.

"No, nothing. There will be nothing."

"An orange Hedi and I can split? Or walnuts? A doll, just a tiny little doll?"

"Nothing, but the camp organizers may come around to sing Christmas carols."

"*Christkindle*?" asks Hedi.

"We'll see."

Our conversation is suddenly interrupted. Clapping her hands, an attendant announces in a booming voice, "Children, line up along both sides of the aisle." From my place at the end of the room, I peep forward eagerly for a glimpse of the flowing white, filmy gown of the Christmas Angel. Instead, I see heavily rouged figures dressed in garish colors from head to toe. One is carrying a long baton with tiny bells wearing a large floppy hat. Another is holding switches in both hands. Terrified, I scream, "Don't let them get me!"

"They won't hurt you," my mother assures me.

"Keep them away!" I scream climbing wildly to the top of my bed. "Get out of here!"

The entertainers stop. "What's wrong with her?" One takes a step toward me. I scream, "Don't hurt me. I've been good. I'll be good!"

"I have candy for you, a nice piece of candy."

"Don't hurt me! Don't hurt me!" I scream repeatedly until my throat is sore.

He motions for the other children to follow him and distributes candy to each outside the room in the hallway. Hedi returns carrying her prize, two brightly wrapped pieces of hard candy.

"Go outside. They're holding some for you."

"No," I shake my head ducking under my blanket for safety.

"Because of you, we didn't get to sing carols. You are such a scaredy-cat," grumbles one of the other children.

"Go get your candy," cajoles my mother. "You'll like the candy. They won't hurt you. They like children. Go on."

"No, I don't like candy." I bury myself deeper in the blanket, sucking my thumb. I wonder wherever the infant is if she is seeing the beautiful Christmas Angel with God.

One of the attendants tugs my blanket. "Here is your candy." She drops two brightly wrapped nuggets onto my blanket. "Now wave to the jester at the door." I shrink back, seeing the waving wand in his hand, making the bells jingle. "He won't come in. Just wave and say thank you."

"*Danke schoen,*" I say, looking at the bright nuggets in my hand. I wave to him at the doorway, where he is waiting for a response.

He waves back, smiling, with a familiar Christmas greeting, "*Froeliche Weihnachten,* Merry Christmas!" I think that this cannot be Christmas because Christmas is a holiday with kissing and hugging family, lots of delicious food, delicate cookies, a warm toasty fire, and lots of presents.

"Boy, you're quite a handful. You really hurt his feelings. He's very sensitive. He only wanted to make the children happy," says the attendant.

Feeling guilty and afraid, I clutch the candy in a tight fist, peering into the attendant's flushed face.

"Eat your candy," she says brusquely stomping out of the room.

Mid-afternoon of Christmas Day, the refugees are told to prepare to leave early the next morning. Those too weak or ill will remain in camp to await their fate.

Chapter Five

"*Do you think the sessions are helping you?*"

"*I guess so. I just have to trust you and God or whatever is guiding us. Our sessions are helping me to recognize where I am in some of the flashbacks. Sometimes I know where I am in the war — on a train, my mother leaving me, bombs...lots of bombs...death of the baby in the camp. I don't know, it all seems too huge, like a gigantic emotional mountain.*"

"*When in a flashback, are you remembering what to do?*"

"*It's like bending steel with my mind and emotions to say that was then and now I'm here safe where there is help. The fear stays with me. At times, the fear leaves me, but it takes super human efforts. How on earth can I live like this? It takes so much effort and energy to separate the past from the present.*"

"*In time it will become easier to be in the present safety of your adult life. To know that the fear you are feeling in the present is because of experiences in your childhood when you were not safe.*"

"*I hope so. I hope so. It just seems impossible...more than I can possibly do. It's very discouraging.*"

"*You are making excellent progress,*" he reassures me.

"*Am I? Do you really see moments of healing?*" I ask anxiously.

"*Yes. I really do. You've made great progress in just a few months. Your memories are very close to the surface of your awareness. Do you know what triggers your flashbacks?*"

"*Not really. Well, maybe one. When I hear trains whistle with the rhythmic clickity-clacking of wheels.*"

~ ~ ~ ~ ~ ~

*T*he train pulls deeper into Germany. Now airplanes often unload their deadly cargo onto the railroad tracks, and staccato machine guns from the sky strafe the trains. When we reach our destination, we are housed with the Heller family in a small, second-story apartment that has been vacated by its residents. The Heller's three children are Otto, the oldest, Adeltraud, and little Siegfried. *Mutti* and *Frau* Heller become close friends. Often they search together for food, clothing, and firewood. One night, the mothers discuss our survival problems around the wooden kitchen table.

"Look," *Mutti* says, "there is no other solution. We have to get wood from the forest. It's too cold to be without a fire. We only have enough wood for two more days."

"Oh, no, not that again," says *Frau* Heller's husband. "I can't take it. Last time, I almost died of fright."

"How can you talk like that, Adam? You're the man. Or are you a mouse?" teases my mother.

"A mouse, I admit it. Don't you ever get scared? You seem to have nerves of steel."

"Sure, I'm scared a lot, but we need the wood. There is no other choice."

"She's right, Adam," says his wife. "We need to keep warm. And the townspeople won't give us any firewood."

"You're as bad as Kathe. Think of our children if we get caught."

"I'm afraid too," says *Frau* Heller. "They've beefed up their patrols. Now they shoot first and ask questions later. Do you have a plan, Kathe?"

Pretending to be asleep, I listen as they make their plans, with fear mounting in my heart.

"It has to be at night," says *Mutti*. "Gertie, you be the lookout. If you hear anything, we'll stop, and throw ourselves on the ground." Pulling closer together, they giggle. "Boy, aren't we the spies?"

"Adam, you're the man. You're the strongest. You chop down the trees, and I'll stack them on Siegfried's little wagon," continues *Mutti*.

"You should have been a man, Kathe. You have more courage than any man I know," says Adam in admiration. The women suppress their smiles.

"But," he continues, "you can't just trot down the road pulling a wagon into the forest. Somebody will get suspicious. Last time we were lucky; we found a pile of firewood near the edge."

He considers. "I could pretend to go for a walk during the day and pick out some dead trees. We'll carry the wagon there so it won't make any noise. On the way back, we'll have to walk across the fields and follow the creek. The banks are frozen. We should be able to pull the wagon over the ground easily. The trees should muffle any sounds, and keep us fairly hidden." He pauses again. "This is insane. How did you ever talk me into this? If we don't get caught, our children will tell their children of this escapade."

"We'll go at midnight. Don't tell the children," says my mother.

The next morning, when Hedi starts the fire, she is surprised at what she sees. She rushes into the house, and awakens her sleeping mother. "Wake up, wake up, our wood pile is filled; somebody filled it up during the night!"

"I know."

"Did you get it? How?"

"Gertie, Adam, and I got it from the forest."

Hedi gasps.

"Don't worry, no one saw us. Don't tell anyone. I'm tired. Take care of your sister. How much food do we have? Enough for today?"

"Yes, but for today only; maybe a little for tomorrow," answers Hedi anxiously.

"Fine. *Frau* Heller and I'll find something tomorrow. Now let me sleep. Try to be quiet." *Mutti* sleeps all day. When she gets up toward evening, she eats the boiled potato and sips the hot cup of tea that Hedi has prepared for her.

Early the next morning, while we children are still in bed, the two mothers leave in search of food.

"Put on your coats, hats, and scarves," orders Hedi. "We're going for a walk." Adeltraud, Siegfried, and I scramble to tug on our warmest clothes.

"Are we going to the train?" I ask Hedi anxiously. "We can't leave. *Mutti* isn't here."

"*Frau* Heller and *Mutti* are looking for food. They'll be home later. We're just going out to play," says Hedi. Otto and Hedi tie 1aces and help us younger children to button our coats.

"I don't want to go outside. It's cold," I whine. "I don't like being cold."

"You're going outside. The fresh air will be good for you," answers Hedi briskly.

Outside, we three younger children huddle together against the lashing wind. We reluctantly follow Hedi and Otto ahead of us. I overhear them engaged in serious conversation, stopping on the middle of a bridge built over the creek. Gloomily they look down at the ice below. In the middle of the creek, water gurgles, pushing against the unrelenting icy walls.

"What are we going to do if they don't come back?" asks Hedi. The thought of *Mutti* not returning strikes fear in my heart.

"I guess we'll have to take care of the younger children. Something must have happened. They've never been gone so long before." Otto swallows hard, as if to rid himself of the lump of emotions stuck in his throat.

"Look at them," says Hedi. They both turn toward us younger children standing close to each other on the bank of the creek, too afraid to cross the bridge. She shouts to us, "Chase each other, play tag, you'll be warmer." No one moves. "Go on. Do as I say," she adds, trying to sound grown up. Then in a flat, monotone voice coming from deep inside her throat, she says to Otto, "They'll die without us. But you and I could make it by ourselves." Otto nods in agreement.

"We only have a little food for tonight. How can we feed all of us? And they're always whining. Sometimes they cry, and they don't even know why." She pauses and says again, "Without us, they'll die."

"They'll come home. They always have before. Remember last week how late they were," says Otto, trying not to give in to his panic. His words gave me a sliver of hope that *Mutti* will return.

"No, never this late. Look, the sun is almost gone. It's getting dark. We have to start making plans," Hedi says sensibly. "If we keep our coats on most of the time, we can stretch the firewood for a while, but food is a problem."

"I'm twelve. Almost a man, but you're only ten," he says.

"You may be twelve, but you're far from a man. Anyway, I'm as tall as you. I can run faster than you, and jump farther too," she reminds him.

They pull their heads deeper into their collars. They look at the open space at the other end of the bridge. Then they turn and walk slowly back across toward us. A gently falling snow envelops them as they approach us in the darkness.

At home, Hedi and Otto make hot tea and serve each of us a slice of bread spread with the last of the lard. After dinner, we change into our nightclothes. Otto and Hedi do not want to frighten us by making us sleep in our overcoats just yet.

"Sit between my legs; I'll comb your hair," says Hedi to me.

"Ouch, ouch, you're hurting me," I wail.

"Hildie! You have sores all over your head again. You'd better tell *Mutti*. You know, you really should comb your own hair to keep the lice out of your hair when *Mutti*'s too busy."

"When is she coming home? Why isn't she home? It's late. I'm afraid."

"She'll be home. She said it might take long because they were going to walk to the next town. They heard they could buy a chicken there," lies Hedi. "Maybe we'll have chicken goulash and dumplings. Wouldn't that be nice?"

I know she is lying, but ask for her assurance all the same. "Are you sure she'll be coming home?"

"Yes. I'm positive. Now go to bed."

Pretending to be asleep in my bed, I watch Hedi and Otto sitting silently across from each other, wrapped in their coats. Soon fatigue overcomes them, and they fall asleep with their heads resting on the red and white checkered oilcloth table covering, waiting.

A thud against the door announces the arrival of the two mothers. Hedi springs up and flings open the door. "You're home!" she exclaims, relieved.

"Yes, we're home. It's cold out there. Make us a hot cup of tea. Look, we have a sausage, four loaves of bread, flour, cheese, potatoes, and even a little bottle of milk. And here is a really nice surprise; two bars of perfumed soap. Here, smell it, Hedi."

Drowsy and relieved that *Mutti* is back, I rest in the blankets with eyes closed as I listen to their talk."Hmmm, nice. Where did you find all this food?"

The two mothers exchange glances and laugh, "Well, it wasn't easy, but at least we have some protein," says *Frau* Heller boisterously. "And, for a special treat, we got two chocolate bars. Why don't you and Otto split one right now and eat it."

Wearily, the women kick off their wet boots and warm their feet near the fire while they sip hot tea. "Were you worried because we were late?"

"Yes," say Hedi and Otto simultaneously.

"How is Hildie?" asks *Mutti*, and I feel comforted by her concern.

"She's got sores all over her scalp again. I couldn't comb her hair because she hurt too much."

"I'll have to wash her hair tomorrow. I wish I knew what causes those sores. Are the sores on her body any better?"

"They're healing. They're not infected."

"I hope she doesn't have lice again. That girl! If there is one louse within ten miles, I swear it always finds her. What about you, Hedi?"

"I'm careful to comb my hair every night with the fine-toothed comb. I put it on the newspaper like you showed me, but I don't think I have any lice."

"The sores on your body any better?"

"Yes, I'm washing them every day. I think the cream is helping. The scabs are falling off. I'm fine."

"How long will we stay in this town?" asks Otto.

"A few weeks at the most, according to the officials. It's really unclear why we have to leave, but we have no choice. We have to do as we're told."

I fall into a deep sleep as their conversation goes on into the late night.

For a few weeks, life is almost normal. The five of us children are often alone while *Frau* Heller and *Mutti* search for food. When the mothers are at home, they mend, brush, and wash all of our clothing. The sores on my scalp and body heal. But little Siegfried's nose never stops running. He seems to have a perpetual cold.

~ ~ ~ ~ ~ ~

Late one evening, both our families lug our baggage to the cold, drafty train depot. With the other refugees, we wait for hours for a train. Once on the train, our progress is constantly halted by unexplained delays. The train organizers walk back and forth along the train arguing with each other. The refugees are told to evacuate the train. After we were all standing on the platform, buffeted by the bitter cold wind and icy pellets, orders are given to return to the same train. The trains are drafty and often unheated.

Especially frightening are the long tunnels carved through mountains. I have heard rumors that tunnels are sometimes filled with lethal gas that kills all the occupants when the trains are forced to stop. On the train, I sit away from the frosted windowpanes because it is too cold. Usually *Mutti* sits near the window, with me in the middle, and Hedi next to me. All three of us are dressed in our hats and coats and wrapped in blankets.

Some days, the moisture from the cold air and warm body temperatures of the passengers cloud the windowpanes inside the train. I watch the rivulets sliding down the pane, momentarily exposing the bleak, overcast, snowy landscape outside. Other times, on crisp sunny days, I sit enthralled for hours, studying the delicate patterns on the icy windowpanes. At times, I am so completely absorbed by the sparkling crystalline beauty that I no longer feel hunger pangs or the sensation of cold in my always-shivering body.

Worried constantly about frostbite, *Mutti* rubs our hands and feet. She makes us blow on our hands and rub them together. Whenever we enter a tunnel, *Mutti* says to us, "Hold your breath. Try not to breathe more than you have to." I try to hold my breath until it feels like my lungs will burst. Then I gulp a breath of air and wait to see if I will die.

One day, the train pulls into a tunnel for safety from the bombers. While the train is stopped, I hold my breath. Then I gulp air a number of times. Finally, I say to *Mutti* in the pitch blackness, "I can't hold my breath anymore. I'm getting dizzy. I don't feel good."

"Just a few more minutes," comes the answer.

A rumbling sound shakes the train. People scream in the total darkness. "Be calm," shouts a male voice over the din. "They're bombing. We're safe in here. We're safe in here."

The people quiet down. Then another voice says in the inky blackness, "I don't know how safe we are. Tunnels seem to be targets for the bombers. You saw the whole mountainside bombed out a few days ago. If there was a train in that tunnel, everyone died."

The crowd murmurs, near panic again. "Don't be ridiculous," says the first voice. "That tunnel was along the edge of the mountain. The one we're in now is deep in the middle of a huge mountain. Bombs can't hurt us here."

"But," says the other voice, "the walls could crack and send rocks down on us and bury us alive."

"Shut up!" says the first voice vehemently. "Keep your cowardice to yourself."

Silence.

"*Mutti*, what does the gas smell like?" I ask.

"I don't know."

"I smell it. Don't you smell it? Does it hurt to die from gas?"

"I don't smell anything. No, there's no pain with gas; it doesn't hurt at all."

"How does it feel? Will it take a long time to die?"

"No. It's so fast you won't even know it happened. There is no pain. Don't worry."

"I smell something!" someone shouts. "Gas, gas, they threw in gas!"

I start to get up, but *Mutti* feels my movement, and reaches out in the blackness. "Sit down, Hildie." She pulls me down. "Hedi, are you there?"

"Yes," says a frightened voice.

"Let me go!" I scream. "It's gas. We'll die!" I strain against my mother's hands.

"Sit down and be quiet," my mother says sternly, her voice tight, deep within her throat. "There is no place to go. We're in total darkness. We can't see. Bombers are outside. Hedi, don't move."

"Don't open your windows. It'll let the gas in," shouts a male voice.

The air grows thicker. Breathing becomes more difficult. "It smells like smoke from a fire," someone shouts. "It must be from the engines. Tell the engineer to shut off his engines."

A door swooshes open. Feet stumble down the stairs. More shouts, "Shut the engine off!"

"It isn't gas. Thank God," says a voice.

"Well, don't be so relieved. Carbon monoxide is deadly." People cough. "Don't sleep. Stay awake."

"The engines are turned off!" The news is shouted along the black tunnel. "It'll take a while for the air to clear, but we're all right now. We won't die." Relieved, I rest my head on *Mutti's* shoulder. For hours, the train hides in the dark, serpentine curves of the tunnel, while the unceasing rain of bombs shakes the mountainside.

Finally, scouts from the tunnel entrance report that the airplanes are gone. When the engines shudder to life, the added emissions make breathing more difficult again; the air had never really cleared in the hours we sat in the darkness. The train whistle hoots a warning for people to return to their seats. When the train pulls out of the tunnel, the people tear open the windows and doors for fresh air. In the clear, starlit night, the train slithers along the tracks through a series of shorter tunnels.

During the next few days, the train moves through daylight and darkness and the intermittent black tunnels. Always there is the hope that at the next stop things will be better. Instead, conditions are becoming worse. Bombings seem to increase steadily.

~ ~ ~ ~ ~ ~

*A*t the next stop, our family is placed into another apartment. A white-haired woman who teaches at the university shows us the beautifully furnished apartment. The modern kitchen is immaculately clean.

"Whose apartment is this?" I ask.

"This belongs to a family that left," answers the woman. We walk into the kitchen. "You may use everything, but use it with respect, since it doesn't belong to you. Are there any appliances you are unfamiliar with? I would be glad to explain their use to you."

"We have modern conveniences at home also," says my mother.

The professor looks doubtful. "Do you know what this is?" she asks.

"No, what is it?" I ask eagerly.

"Just put this rod into a cup of water. Plug it in for a few minutes, and it will make the water hot. See, touch the water. It's warm already."

"Wow, is that great! Isn't that great, *Mutti*?"

"We had one like that at home," says my mother stiffly.

"We did? I don't remember...," but the stiffness in my mother's voice makes me stop talking.

The white-haired professor opens each cabinet and drawer in the gleaming white kitchen, showing my mother where to find things. Never having taken an interest in the kitchen at home, my young mind is astonished by the pots and pans, stove, can opener, and coffee maker. I am aware that my delight and obvious interest is grating on my mother's nerves, but for once, I am so exuberant that I am barely concerned about *Mutti*'s silent, stern looks.

"This is the living room, which will be your room. The bedroom may be occupied by another family later. I told the officials I didn't want anyone here, but they insisted." She opens the white lace curtains of the double French doors to a lovely warm room. Hedi and I are overjoyed. We touch the gleaming mahogany armoire. The sparkling moss-green-tiled stove has deliciously warm walls. Heavy lace curtains cover the ceiling-to-floor windows, and a thick, deep, rich, multicolored rug covers the floor.

"Where are the people?" I ask again.

"They're gone, but they'll be back. They sent us a postcard. See?" She pulls a postcard from the pocket of her sweater and shows it to my mother. *Mutti* reads and returns it.

"But when are they coming back? Why would they leave now? Are they afraid of the Russians? Won't they mind if we use their things?" I cannot grasp why they would have left.

"You may use their things, but use them carefully. I promised to take care of their belongings. I have until now, but the officials forced me to take you in."

"Why are they gone? Where are they?" To me, it is incomprehensible that anyone would leave such a nice, warm home.

"Are they Jews?" my mother asks, placing her hand compassionately on the older woman's arm.

"Yes, they are my friends." Tears well up in her eyes, her face flushed. "When they return, they'll find their things just as they left them." The women exchange uncomfortable glances. "I had to let you use this apartment. Don't tell anyone I said that they were my friends," she says frightened.

"But why did they leave?" I ask again, still not understanding.

"They had to leave because they're Jews."

"Is that what's been happening?" asks *Mutti* .

"Yes. One day they're here, and the next day they're gone in an instant. Jews—and many other Germans—just disappear. One has to be very careful what one says."

"That isn't right. Surely, they must have broken the law or done something wrong," says my mother.

"No. They lived good lives and obeyed the laws. You're new here. It isn't safe to speak so openly." The other woman lowers her voice. "Don't trust anyone. Be sure to tell your children. I have to go now. Let me know if I can help you. I have very little food, but I'll bring you up some sandwiches and hot cocoa."

After the woman is gone, we take off our coats and warm ourselves by the fire. "I still don't know where the family is. Why did they go?" I had to understand.

"They must have been forced to leave."

"Like us?"

"I don't know what happened here. All I know is that they're Jews. Be careful here, girls."

"But what does being Jewish have to do with leaving? I'll bet they were afraid of the Russians," I say.

"Don't ask so many questions. You learn more by listening. Listen and observe. And, for heaven's sake, never, NEVER, mention Jews again. It's unsafe. Understand?"

"Yes," I reply, but I do not understand.

A few days later, Hedi and I attend school. I am painfully shy. The children make fun of my dialect. When a man walks into the room, his three-piece suit hanging down from his skinny shoulders and his loosely fitting pants cinched tightly at the waist, the children sit erect in their seats, hands folded on their desks, and feet together, firmly planted on the floor. No one makes a sound. I stand near the wall in the middle of the room.

"So, you're the new refugee child. What's your name?" says the teacher, easing his scarecrow body on the top of the desk. All eyes are on me.

"Hildie Weiler."

"Hildie. Is that your name, or is it a nickname?"

"Hildegard Weiler."

The teacher's eyes slide over my shabby clothes and scuffed shoes. "Sit in the empty seat in front of you. Can you read?"

I remain silent and hang my head.

"Hildegard Weiler, please read page 37."

"I don't have a book."

"What kind of language is that you're speaking? Surely it can't be German. Can't you speak high German? Where are you from?"

"Hungary."

One of the other students slips a book in front of me.

"Please read out loud," orders the teacher. I stare at the book."How old are you?"

"Seven. No, eight."

"Well, which is it? Don't you know how old you are?" The children snicker.

"I'm not sure," I stammer. More snickers.

The teacher rolls his eyes, "Surely you don't call that German. I can hardly understand you. Are there any other students who can't understand Hildegard?" Most of the students raise their hands. "There's no sense in reading, since no one can understand you anyway. Stephan, please read page 37 from the top."

I sigh a sigh of relief. My head down on my chest, I am miserable.

"Take out your pencils and paper. Hildegard, where are you writing materials? You mean your mother sent you to school without pencil and paper? Don't you have paper and pencils in your schools in Hungary?"

"Yes, but…"

"But what? Surely your mother didn't send you to school and expect you to learn without a ruler, pencil, or paper," he says contemptuously.

I am suddenly furious. "My mother is too busy getting food and taking care of my sister and me. You're the teacher. It's your job to teach me."

"What a fresh mouth. Does your mother let you talk like that at home?"

"You leave my mother alone!" I raise my voice angrily. "You have no right to speak about my mother. If she had school supplies, I would have them. We lost everything in our journey. Leave my mother alone."

A shocked silence pervades the classroom. "Tomorrow you will have a pencil and paper, or do not come into my class," he says coldly.

At home, I say stubbornly, "I'm not going back to school, ever."

"What happened?" asks *Mutti.*

"The teacher said I couldn't come back unless I have a pencil and paper. He is so mean. He doesn't like me and the children don't like me either."

"Where am I going to get paper and pencil? I have no money for school supplies."

"I know."

"The teacher gave me my supplies as soon as I got there," says Hedi. "I like school. Didn't your teacher have anything for you?"

"No. I can't come back without them. I can't go back. I have forgotten how to read. The other kids are such good readers," my voice cracks.

"You have to get an education. That's something that can't be taken from you. No one can take what's in your head; it's always with you," says *Mutti.*

Just then, a knock on the door. "Come in."

"Good evening," says the professor. "Why, what's the matter? Why is the little one so sad?" I pour out my tale to the kindly woman, who listens intently. She consoles me, "Don't be hurt by the teacher. The war has changed all of us. I'll bring you supplies. Do try to learn how to speak high German. All educated people learn to speak it."

"I'm not going back to that mean man and kids," I say with a little less force.

"You talk it over with your mother. I just came to tell you that another family will be moving into the bedroom next to you. You will be sharing the kitchen. You have taken such good care of everything. It's quite a responsibility taking care of other people's belongings."

"We'll watch out for them. Nothing will be ruined," assures my mother.

Hedi and I play with the dolls and clothes we found deep in a corner in the bottom of the armoire.

"You found their dolls?" says the professor. "You girls are being careful, aren't you? They loved their dolls. Their parents lavished them with the finest. They even had a seamstress sew doll clothes. That doll is the size of an infant. In fact, that outfit you're taking off belonged to a baby down the street. Why are you undressing the dolls?"

"We're going to wash them."

"Why? They aren't dirty. They were nice, clean, little girls."

"We have to wash them so they won't get boils or lice."

"What?" she says shocked.

Our mother throws her hands in the air and shakes her head, "Oh, for heavens sake. Can't you two forget the war even when you're playing?" The women leave to have tea downstairs with the professor's husband.

Hedi and I bathe the dolls in the bathroom, dry them, and pretend to put salve on their bodies. I hug and cradle the doll the way I had seen the young mother care for her baby in the refugee camp.

Evenings, after school, and on weekends Hedi and I play with the dolls, reliving our moments as refugees. Our former lives in Hungary no longer seem to exist.

After school one day, Hedi walks with me back to the apartment. As usual, I am withdrawn, "Is it getting any better at school?" asks Hedi.

"No," I say, kicking a clump of snow as we walk.

"What's he done now?"

"Nothing. He ignores me, as if I wasn't even there. The kids don't like me either."

"Do they ask you to play with them during recess?"

"Yes, but I don't."

"Why not?"

"Why should I play with them? They don't really like me. I'll never forget how they laughed at me. My clothes aren't nice. We're poor, aren't we?"

"No, we are not," says Hedi firmly. "It's just that everything we own is in Hungary. We're richer than most of the kids in school. Father has two butcher shops and an export business and *Mutti* has a clothing store. Don't ever think you're poor." The shrill air raid sirens interrupt our conversation.

"Oh, no, not another air raid." We grab hands and flee to the nearest air raid shelter. We sit together in the bunker, not knowing where *Mutti* is or if she is still alive. The earth of the bunker shakes as the bombs hit their target. A few hours later the siren shrieks, announcing that the danger had passed.

Anxiously we race toward home. "Oh, no. They bombed a house here. Only a half block away from where we live," says Hedi. Our hearts pound. Holding hands, we run until we see our house. We bolt into the apartment, but *Mutti* is not there.

"You stay here and wait for *Mutti*. I'll try to find her," says Hedi.

"Don't leave me alone. Please don't!" I shriek.

"You'll be safe here. I promise I'll be back."

"Don't go. Please don't go."

"I have to. She may be hurt. I have to help her. Stay by the window until I get back," Hedi says as she runs down the stairs. From the street below, Hedi waves to me as I press against the window, my face contorted with silent sobs. After a while, I stop crying. Sucking my thumb, I force myself to calm down by praying, "God, please let my mother and sister be all right. Please, God, let them be all right. Please, God, please, God."

"Where's Hedi?" *Mutti* had returned, but I was too absorbed in my prayers to hear her.

"Oh, *Mutti*! I'm so glad you're home!" I run to my mother and hug her.

"Where's Hedi? Did she come home from school with you?"

"Here I am. I'm fine," says Hedi as she comes through the door. "We were worried about you, so I went to look for you."

"How many times do I have to tell you not to go out so soon after an air raid? It isn't good for you to see those things. Did you see the building near here?" *Mutti* asks Hedi.

"Yes."

"I wish you hadn't seen that." *Mutti* pulls a big suitcase toward the middle of the room. "We have to start packing. We're leaving tomorrow. I hope we can go somewhere where there aren't so many air raids."

"I wish we could stay. I like this apartment. I like school. My lessons in reading and arithmetic are going so well. I've made friends," says Hedi.

"I know. It's always hard leaving friends. I miss the Hellers, too. When this war is over, we'll have friends again." She starts pulling out clothes and luggage.

"Can we take the dolls?" I ask. I have no regrets about leaving. I hate going to school.

"No. You know they're keeping them safe for the other little girls. Although I doubt they'll ever return." When everything is packed, Hedi and I put layer after layer of tiny doll clothes on the dolls.

"What are you girls doing with those dolls?" asks the professor, as she enters the room.

"We're playing refugee exodus," answers Hedi.

"You're not thinking of taking those dolls, are you? They don't belong to you."

"We know they're not ours," I say.

That night, we tuck the dolls under our arms while we sleep. The next day, we wait all day for the army van to pick us up. In a hushed voice, I say to Hedi, "We can't take them. You heard the professor. They're not ours."

"You heard *Mutti*," replies Hedi. "Those girls won't be back. If they do come back, there are three other dolls. We're only going to take two. Just slip your doll under your coat. No one will notice."

"I do love this doll. She looks just like a real baby. I wish I could keep her."

Late at night, the van finally comes. After the baggage is loaded, our family hops on the back. It is bitter cold. The stars sparkle like diamonds. As soon as the canvas flaps of the van are closed, Hedi and I exchange triumphant smiles. "When they notice that two dolls are missing, we'll be far away," whispers Hedi.

"Halt! Halt!" shouts a man's voice. The canvas flap flies open. "There they are, the thieves! You should be ashamed, *Frau* Weiler. After my wife and I befriended you. The thanks we get is that you steal those dolls."

"I don't have your dolls. Look through our luggage if you don't believe me," says *Mutti*, highly indignant.

He glares at us. "I don't have to look at your luggage. Here is a doll and there is the other." He grabs the dolls from underneath our coats. "Where are the other ones?"

"We only took two," says Hedi.

"We thought you were well-mannered children, but all of you are only thieving, lying gypsies," he fumes, completely out of control.

"How can you begrudge those dolls to my children? I didn't know they had them, but what harm is there in giving them a little joy? I haven't seen them this happy in a long time," says our mother.

"Let them have the dolls," says the soldier.

"The dolls don't belong to them. They stole them."

Mutti retorts, "They don't belong to you either. You and I know that the owners will probably never return. If they do, they wouldn't be so selfish; they would share. There are other dolls in the armoire."

The man holds the two dolls, one under each arm. His unending tirade is interrupted by the soldier who pushes him aside. Before fastening the canvas flap, the soldier smiles and winks at Hedi and me. The caravan of army vans loaded with refugees advances to the train station.

Chapter Six

*T*hrough the glass of the French doors, I watch a cat prowl silently on the porch behind Dr. Gregg. For some reason, it makes me uncomfortable. The doctor watches my face, then glances around at the cat.

"Do you not like the cat?" he asks.

I don't know what to say.

"Tell me," he insists.

"No, you love that cat," I say. I hesitate.

"Actually, it's my wife's cat," he says.

"It is the ugliest cat I have ever seen." I feel an abnormal resentment toward the cat.

He considers my declaration for several moments. He notices my extreme discomfort.

"Why didn't you want to tell me you don't like the cat? Are you protecting me?" he asks.

Immediately his suggestion strikes a chord in me.

"I don't want to hurt your feelings," I blurt out. "Sometimes I can tell you are visibly shaken by my war experiences." Suddenly, I am overwhelmed by a sense of concern. I am alarmed at the impact that I fear my experiences are having on him.

"I know how to take care of myself after you leave. I have 10 – 15 minutes between patients. This is your time. Think only of yourself. Don't hold back to protect me."

Somehow his words reassure me.

~ ~ ~ ~ ~ ~

*T*he train jerks to a halt amid green meadows dotted with yellow wildflowers. People press close to the windows, straining to see a train depot or an oncoming train. They discuss reasons why the train stopped. Shortly, four men from the train, dressed in drab, threadbare jackets and slacks, walk quickly past the window toward the front of the train. The leader, his gray cap pulled down sideways over his right eye, swings his arms in cadence with his rapid pace. The tightly clustered group moves as one, their shoulders almost touching, following the leader.

No one seems to notice the golden afternoon sun. After a while, a few children dash to the side of the meadow, pull down their pants and squat. Their modesty is momentarily lost in the delight of relieving themselves in the fresh air of nature. If at all possible, the refugees avoid the stench of urine, diarrhea, and vomit in the restrooms on board the trains. Adults join the children, but turn their backs to the ever-probing eyes at the windows. Hedi joins the others outside to play tag. But I am tired and hungry, and running seems too exhausting. Instead, I join two boys who are kicking gravel pebbles along the railroad ties.

"Why do you think we stopped?" I ask them.

"Don't know," answers the taller boy. "Don't see a train depot. No other train tracks." He squints and looks at the sky. "Can't see any airplanes." The smaller boy and I look up apprehensively.

"There could be bombers, and we just can't see them yet," I say. "You know how often they surprise us. All of a sudden they're here, shooting at us."

"Yeah," he agrees glumly as he kicks another pebble. The other boy is smaller than I. He looks frantically at the sky, at me, and at the older boy. In silence, they stroll back and forth along the train, trying to comprehend amid the sounds of adults loudly deliberating the cause for the delay. Boisterous children chase each other, the gravel crunching under their worn shoes.

"I don't hear airplanes," says the little boy anxiously.

"That's right. We always hear the bombers before we see them," says the older boy. He stands still listening. "Do you hear anything?"

All three of us stop and listen. I say, "No. I don't think I hear bombers, but there is so much noise, maybe we can't hear them. Quiet!" I shout. "Quiet!" we all shout in unison.

"Do you hear planes?" asks a woman, anxiously peering into the sky. She shouts, "Quiet! Listen for airplanes." Within an instant, all talking and crunching of feet cease abruptly. Some even hold their breath, searching the cobalt-blue sky. The group of four men, who had walked by before, crunch into the circle of silence. "What's going on?" demands the man with the cap.

"We're listening for airplanes," several answer. All become silent again.

"There are no planes. Go back to what you were doing," he snaps, as the group continues their stomping on crunchy gravel.

"How long will we be here?" shouts someone after the group. The leader only shrugs his shoulders without interrupting his determined pace.

"That man could be wrong, you know. Remember how many times we don't hear the planes until they start to shoot at us? All of a sudden we hear ra-ta-tat-ta, ra-ta-tat-ta, and see orange sparks from the sky," I say to the older boy, still troubled.

The boy looks at me and nods in agreement. We stand facing each other, dropping our heads as we watch the others kicking pebbles.

"I've got it. The reason we often can't hear the airplanes is because the locomotive engines are running and make a lot of noise," says the older boy gleefully.

Grinning and relieved, I say, "You're right! We could hear a bomber now because the engines aren't running." We laugh, moving our arms back and forth, imitating the train.

Just then, the man with the cap slips behind us and crawls underneath the train. "What are you doing?" we ask, bending to follow him. Scrunched in an uncomfortable position, he examines every crevice under the car, "I'm looking for bombs on this train," he says distractedly as he scrambles over the gravel. "Nothing here." Within an instant he is gone, leaving us alone underneath the train car.

Looking around at this dark world, the younger boy begins to whimper, "I'm afraid."

"Let's get out of here," says the older boy, grabbing his brother's shoulder. Quickly they stumble out into the fading afternoon light. "Hildie, come out," he calls to me.

"No. I like it here. I'm staying. Leave me alone."

"I'm gonna tell your mother. Come over here."

"I don't care if you tell her. I just want to stay here for a little while. I'll be out soon. Leave me alone." I kneel on a crosstie and look around. For the first time in what seemed like a lifetime, I am alone, all alone. For a moment, the sounds fade. All is silent for me. Looking up I see black-pitted grease on cylindrical forms, giant nuts and bolts, and straight pieces of steel solidly connected. Glancing down, I see shiny steel tracks on either side of me bolted to strong wooden beams. I relax my body across the gray rough beams and white gravel. I imagine steel bars along the open sides, protecting me from the nightmare outside. I feel safe in the filtered darkness, and so tired. My gravel mattress feels soft and comforting. I am reminded of home.

"Get out from under there. What are you doing?" says a gruff male voice.

"I'm. . . , I'm. . .," I stutter.

"Get over here this instant, this minute," demands the man as he sticks his white-haired head under the train car.

Quickly, I stand up in a bent position, starting to examine one part of the underside of the train. Then I peer into a corner near a cylindrical shape, getting black grease on my hands. I say to the man, "I'm looking for a bomb. Nope. No bombs here. I'll be out in a minute. I have to check a few more places."

"You come out here this minute, or I'm going to come under there to get you," says the old man threateningly, and painfully he begins to crawl under the train.

"I'm coming, I'm coming," I say as I crawl back into the din of the crowd of people standing near the stopped train. I see dark figures silhouetted against a vermilion sunset.

The old man's face is red from anger and the strain of getting up from his hands and knees. He says to me, "Don't you ever go underneath a train again. It's too dangerous."

"No, I was safe, really safe. Come, I'll show you."

"What if the train jerked and you were on the tracks? And what's this nonsense about looking for bombs? Do you know what a bomb looks like?" I shake my head. He continues, "No, of course not. Leave the search for bombs to the men. You might find one and get hurt."

I pinch my lips tightly together to keep from telling him that it would have been fine with me if a bomb had exploded while I lay in that quiet spot on the gravel. Having made his point, the old man stomps off. The train whistles; people scramble to get back onto the train.

When *Mutti* asks me how my hands got so greasy, I answer, "I don't know." I know my mother will be upset if I tell her about the peaceful place underneath the train.

~ ~ ~ ~ ~ ~

*W*e arrive in a city late at night. As usual, housing is quite a distance from the train depot. Our mother gives Hedi and me valises and coats to carry, while she takes the heaviest suitcases herself. My irregular footsteps scrape the sidewalk as I stumble after *Mutti* and Hedi.

"Hildie, hurry up. You're falling too far behind," yells *Mutti*, straining under the weight of the heavy suitcases.

Half-heartedly, I increase my pace, aware only of my fatigue. I hate the burden of carrying our belongings. "I'm tired," I whine.

"We're all tired," says Hedi, staggering under the weight of her load.

"It's too heavy," I complain. "I can't carry this. It's too heavy." Tears well up in my eyes.

My mother puts down her baggage. "Give me your valise. Now all you have left are two coats and this tiny bag. Come on. It's not too far. Just a little farther," she coaxes.

I am totally absorbed in my own inner turmoil. Maybe it's the way I'm carrying these things. If I can tie it on my back, I probably won't feel how heavy it is, I think. I stop to rearrange the small bag over my shoulder.

"Give me a coat. I'll carry it," says Hedi, slipping it between her upper arm and chest. Bracing herself, she picks up her allotted share. "Please stop crying. *Mutti* and I can't carry more. We're tired, too."

I try hard to swallow my tears and to keep up. I am always falling behind. Our mother turns around as she trudges uphill, "Are you all right, Hedi?"

"Yes, *Mutti*, I'm fine. Is it much farther? Everybody passed us up. Hildie keeps falling behind," she says, worried. Hedi never complains. She recognizes how difficult it is for *Mutti* to keep us alive. She accepts the responsibility of caring for me, though there is only two years' difference in our ages.

"Let's take a rest and let Hildie catch up," says *Mutti* .

Hanging my head on my chest, I catch up and sit on a suitcase to rest. The corners of my mouth are drawn down, and my chest aches from the strain of suppressing my desire to scream.

After a few minutes, *Mutti* says we need to continue. She picks up the baggage, including my share, but I am too lost in my own thoughts to notice. Automatically I get up and start to walk as if in a daze. Each step up the hill is agony for me. "It's too heavy. I can't carry it. It's just too heavy for me," I sob.

Mutti says, "Hildie, look at yourself. You aren't carrying a thing. Nothing. Hedi and I have it all," Hedi and *Mutti* smile at my reaction, as my empty arms search my shoulders and back and pat my body.

"Did I lose it?" I say, confused by the smile shared between my sister and mother.

"No. You didn't lose anything. Why are you always complaining? Look at Hedi. She's tired, but she never complains. You have to stop being such a baby and help us," says *Mutti*.

Feeling foolish and chastised, I cast down my eyes. I do not even notice the determined pace of my steps because I am so angry. No matter what my mother says, I know that the weight I am expected to carry is too heavy for my size. No one could possibly be as tired as I am.

Glad to be off the filthy, noisy train, we three fall into an exhausted sleep in a large building filled with other refugees.

~ ~ ~ ~ ~ ~

The next morning is a crystal clear day. The three of us search for stores or farmers to sell us food. The city sidewalks are alive with people engaged in similar pursuits. Long lines have formed in front of stores that were not bombed. Ration stamps have been given to the refugees, but finding food, clothes, soap, shoes, medicine, and coal or wood for stoves requires endless deliberation and scheming to outwit other people. Most of each day is spent in this manner. The black market is a way of life, even though it is against the law. Being caught carries severe punishment for both the buyer and the seller.

While *Mutti* and Hedi argue with a middle-aged man about the cost of a loaf of bread, which he held concealed in a deep pocket of the inner lining of his coat, I study the milling crowd and the gaping wounds of the bombed-out buildings. I note the different shapes of the bombed buildings. I am particularly interested in a building that was completely bombed, except for the front wall of bricks. The wooden window and doorframes stand precariously without support. I stare at the cerulean blue sky visible through the windows without panes of glass.

Suddenly, air raid sirens wail again. People run and shout. Hurriedly, the middle-aged man with the bread takes the money, and *Mutti* sticks the loaf of bread into a loosely woven shopping bag. People jostle the three of us as *Mutti* grabs our hands, starting to race back to the building reserved for refugees. Within a few seconds, the city streets are completely empty.

The air raid warden shouts over the sirens to our mother, motioning toward a brick structure. Confused, *Mutti* continues in the opposite direction. I see the man motioning frantically with one hand. With the other, he turns a large circle of steel, forcing out a concealing fog. The sirens pierce our ears. Now a white fog makes it almost impossible to see. Leaving his fog-making machine, the air raid warden runs to us, grabs our mother's shoulder, and points toward the bomb shelter. *Mutti* shakes her head. The blinding fog burns our nostrils and eyes. "Get in the shelter. Soon this city will be completely filled with fog. You won't be able to see a thing," he shouts gruffly in her ear. He grabs Hedi's hand and we four run toward the bomb shelter, now barely discernible in the swirling fog.

People stand aside at the entrance to let us in. "Everybody get back, away from the entrance," shouts the air raid warden, herding everyone deeper into the dimly lit caverns. Inside, people sit in total silence on wooden benches. Some sit on the damp floors in the overcrowded shelter. Crashing sounds buffet our ears. The dim, bare light bulbs flicker, and the ground shakes as *Mutti*, Hedi, and I sit huddled together in a terrified grip. I squeeze my eyes shut as I bury my face in the left arm of *Mutti*'s navy-blue wool coat, taking frightened, shallow breaths. Everyone sits in silence, motionless, barely breathing, waiting.

After a while, the air raid warden says, "It sounds like the bombers are past us for now. Hopefully, they won't save a few bombs for us on their return flight."

People start to talk quietly. Children whimper, instinctively knowing not to cry loudly. Some stand up to stretch their cramped, tense muscles.

"Are you cold, Hildie?" asks *Mutti*.

"Yes," I answer through chattering teeth, clutching my knees under my chin to control my shivering body.

My mother opens her wool coat and slips her arms out of the sleeves. Spreading the coat on the floor, she pulls me close to her, wrapping my thin body. She digs in the net shopping bag for the bread and offers me a piece, but I shake my head and clench my jaws so that my mother could not hear my chattering teeth.

"Try to eat it, Hildie. It will make you warmer," she says, shoving a piece into my hand. Turning, she gives Hedi a piece also. Nibbling on a crumb, Hedi tries to swallow.

"Are you all right, Hedi?" asks *Mutti*. Hedi nods her head, but the terror in her sad, brown eyes belies the emotion. Looking away from Hedi's eyes, *Mutti* hangs her head between her bent knees, crossing her arms over her brown hair. Silent tears slide down her cheeks.

"Eat the bread, *Mutti*," says Hedi gently, patting *Mutti*'s back.

For hours, we sit in these cramped positions. Hedi and I fall into merciful sleep, leaning against our mother, who stares vacantly ahead.

Cocking his head to the side at the entrance, the air raid warden says, "Here come the planes. They sound empty. Maybe we'll be spared another bombing."

The shrill air raid siren sounds. "All's clear. You can go to your homes, if they're still standing," says the warden.

The fresh air is welcome as we three slowly walk up the hill holding hands.

~ ~ ~ ~ ~ ~

*E*arly the next morning, *Mutti* awakens Hedi and me. "Hurry. We have to find food before the others get up," she urges us. Sleepily, we pull on the coats that had served as our blankets while we slept.

A fine mist hangs in the air, and milling people again fill the streets. As we stand in line in front of a store, *Mutti* slips us the remaining chunks of bread from her coat pockets. Feeling guilty, with our eyes downcast, we eat while other children watch us enviously.

We are in a different part of the city now. I watch the people sort through the rubble of bombed homes. Very few buildings are undamaged. Inside the store, our mother uses ration cards to procure 100 grams of cheese and a stale loaf of bread. She argues loudly that her children need milk, soap, and medicine for the sores on our bodies. Begrudgingly, she is given milk and a bar of soap. Just as we step through the doorway, the air raid siren begins to wail. *Mutti* grabs a woman's arm and shouts, "Where is the nearest bomb shelter?"

"Follow me," the woman shouts back.

Running through the thickening manmade fog, we hold on to our mother's coat. She carries our precious food supplies. The fog and mist make breathing difficult, but we follow the woman into the shelter.

"Thank you," gasps *Mutti* to the woman as we sit down on a bench.

"You're welcome. You're not from here, are you? Where are you from?" the woman asks, as she pulls her woolen scarf from her blonde hair.

"We're from Hungary. Well, sometimes it's Yugoslavia. The borders change every few years," answers *Mutti*.

"You're quite a long way from home. You speak German very well. Your girls are nice. What are their names?"

"Hedwig and Hildegard and my name is Katherine."

"Those are nice German names. My name is Gertrude."

"Have you had a lot of bombings in this city?"

"Yes. Every day now for weeks. Sometimes twice in one day. Food is getting scarce. This used to be such a beautiful city."

"Here they come," shouts the air raid warden. Silent and motionless we wait.

"They're gone. They didn't drop any bombs." The people cheer.

"Why do they fog the city? It can't be healthy. It burns our lungs and eyes. Makes breathing difficult," says *Mutti* to Gertrude.

"Today was awful. Maybe the mist with the fog made it sting. On clear days, the fog helps confuse the pilots so they can't find our factories and railroad stations."

"Probably we didn't get bombed because of the mist. More than likely they are flying in the sunlight, above the clouds, to another city. I don't like being in bomb shelters, but in this city, it's a necessity," says our mother.

While the women chat, I watch the droplets of water forming between the bricks in the ceiling. This is a bigger shelter than any I have seen before. There are several rooms and dark corridors. The bare light bulbs dimly light the centers of the rooms, leaving the corners in darkness. Although frightened of the shadows, my curiosity motivates me to explore. Cautiously, I take a few steps from my mother, and look back. "It's okay; you can look," *Mutti* says.

Reassured, I step closer to the haze of moisture coating the walls. On one wall, a dull sliver of light glistens faintly. With my fingertips, I touch the glistening spot, but it disappears into tiny icy rivulets down my hand. Disappointed by the lack of prisms, I sigh. I feel a deep emptiness within. Hesitating, I take small cautious steps toward another room. The smudge of light creates eerie figures who sit on the benches watching me. I take a few more uncertain steps into another room. It is half vacant except for a few silent figures sitting in dark corners. Disoriented by the darkness, I am confused by the openings to several rooms, and unsure in which my mother is.

I gasp as a hand touches my shoulder. "What's the matter? Are you lost?" asks my mother.

"No, I knew you were over there," I say.

"Where?" asks *Mutti.*

"Over there," I wave one hand over my shoulder vaguely, gripping my mother's hand with the other.

Back with Hedi and *Mutti,* I lay down on the bench on my back. Looking at the ceiling, I see a narrow rectangle of a grayish blue. "*Mutti,* what's that?" I ask. She looks to where I point.

"Those are air holes."

"Why is it that color?"

"It's the sky you see. It must be clearing up."

"No. It can't be outside."

"Yes, it is."

Lying on my back, I look at the rectangle. I am drawn to it like a magnet. For hours, I stare at the light imagining that I could slip through the rectangle. I fall asleep.

When I wake up, I can't see the light. "*Mutti,* it's gone! We won't get air. The hole is gone. Did a bomb cover it?" I shake my mother's arm.

"No. It isn't gone. It's night, and the sky is black. We're still getting air. Don't worry."

"Get away from the entrance," shouts the air raid warden. "The planes are coming back. They're still loaded. They must have had bad weather in Berlin."

The rumbling intensifies. Muffled explosions increase to thundering crashes that shake the bunker. "Oh, my God," cry the men at the entrance, as flashes of light create silhouettes of their bodies against the darkness. "This is going to be bad. We can't survive a direct hit." Debris flies into the entrance way. Another sharp crash hits near the shelter.

"Ohhhh," the people gasp in unison. The light flickers and goes out. Sitting in the blackness for a long time, my hands dig into the palm of my mother's hand, my frightened body rigidly pulling into a death-like stillness. A man and woman scream, running toward the entrance. The warden does not let them leave. "We don't want to die here in this dark, cold hole. Let us go outside."

"No. You're safer in here. You can't get hurt by flying objects here. If we get a direct hit, it will be over soon enough, but outside, you may get wounded. You must stay," orders the warden. His logic calms the couple. Others pace back and forth near the entrance ready to flee. There are more crashes closer, and some muffled explosions hitting sites farther away.

"Did they get the ammunition factory?" someone asks.

"I think the railroad station was hit."

When the bombings finally end, we leave the shelter.

~ ~ ~ ~ ~ ~

*E*arly the next morning, still dressed in the same clothes from the day before, we are awakened by our mother. "I want you girls to stay here. Don't leave our suitcases alone for a minute. Stay awake. You can drink this milk and eat a small piece of bread. I'm going to find out when the next train leaves. We have to get out of this city. Don't eat more than I said, because I may not be able to get more food. We have to get out of this place," she says again. "Be good, girls. Hedi, watch Hildie, and try to pack our things so we can leave as soon as I return."

"What if the bombers come? What should I do?" asks Hedi. "Should we run for the bomb shelter?"

"No, just stay here. There won't be bombers this early, I hope. I'll be back. I promise," says *Mutti* as she picks up her purse and net shopping bag.

After *Mutti* leaves, Hedi and I sit together on the bare wooden floor where we had slept. We pull our tattered blankets around ourselves for warmth. I pull my hat deeper over my eyebrows and begin to doze.

"You can't sleep," says Hedi from her cocoon. "Let's eat."

"I don't want to eat. It's too cold to put my hand outside this blanket. I'm finally warm."

"You heard *Mutti*. Put your coat on." Pause. "Oh, no, you used your coat for a pillow again. Now it'll be all wrinkled."

"I don't care."

"Well, you'll care when they call you a gypsy and won't give you any food."

I lift my head and start to smooth out the wrinkles from my coat. I know Hedi's comments are true. I know my mother would be upset and ashamed of my crumpled appearance, and that hurt even more than the hunger pangs in my stomach. I stand up in the cold, bare room, put on my coat, hoping the wrinkles will disappear before my mother returns. I pull the maroon wool, pressing my hands on the material, trying to iron out the wrinkles. They seem a little smoother to me. The fox fur collar harkens back to a more prosperous time.

"You slept with your shoes on again. That's not good for your feet," Hedi says wearily.

"I was cold."

"Me, too, but I took mine off. Your shoes make the blankets dirty."

"If the sirens go off, I'll be ready to run. You and *Mutti* are always ready before me, and then I have to run with my shoelaces untied."

Rummaging in the large suitcase, Hedi pulls out two tin cups and pours milk into them. She unwraps a grayish cloth from the half loaf of bread left over from yesterday. Carefully she calculates how much we can eat now and how much needs to be saved for later. Too weak to break the hard bread, she searches for the large knife our mother keeps under the covers by her head while we sleep. Placing the knife in the middle of the half loaf, Hedi bangs the palm of her hand down on the handle. The bread cracks a little. With one more thud, it crumbles apart.

Sitting on the floor, completely absorbed in rationing our food, we did not see a tall heavy-set woman watching us. "Is your mother gone?" she asks in a sugary voice. "Did she leave you two little girls all alone?" She eyes the bread. Her fingers twitch as she studies our belongings.

"No. We're not alone. My mother went downstairs to get us some water," Hedi's too-loud voice bounces off the bare walls. Her white-knuckled hand raises the knife slightly as she glares at the woman.

"What's going on here?" asks another woman as she enters the room. In an instant, she understands the scene. "Get out of here, Bertha. Leave these children alone." The heavy woman glances at the two doorways now filled with people talking about what was happening.

"Come on, Bertha," the other woman coaxes, placing her arm on the heavy woman's shoulders, guiding her out of the room. "Eat your bread, girls. No one will disturb you." One by one the people leave the doorways.

Returning to her task, Hedi rations out two heaps of chunks of bread on the blanket. Carefully, she wraps up the remaining pieces and hides them in a suitcase. We sip the milk.

"The milk tastes funny," I say. My uncombed hair has slipped out of my cap, and a tangle of greasy golden strands hangs over my eyes as I look with disappointment at my cup of milk.

"I know, but we have to drink it anyway."

"Are you sure it won't make us sick?"

"It's just buttermilk. That's all. You know how healthy buttermilk is. We need milk for strong bones," says Hedi logically.

Dunking our bread chunks into the spoiled milk, we eat in silence. Still wearing our woolen caps, coats, and leggings, we sit on a heap of blankets surrounded by baggage. When each crumb was meticulously eaten, I search for water to rinse out the cups. Hedi starts to pack. She packs and repacks until finally she is able to snap the locks shut. Pulling all our baggage close together, we lay ourselves over the heap, making sure that each item is covered with a part of our bodies. As we rest, Hedi says, "Don't sleep. Stay awake. Bertha might come back." We wait for our mother to return.

At last, carrying five boiled potatoes and a stick of margarine, *Mutti* strides into the room. Her footsteps ring as they strike the bare floor. Relieved to see her return safely, Hedi and I jump up and hug her, but she brushes us aside as she examines the baggage, making sure the locks are properly closed.

"The railroad station was bombed last night," she announces briskly. "There might be a train leaving from another station on the outskirts of the city. Where is the bread? You didn't eat it all, did you?"

"No. It's in that suitcase where it's safe," answers Hedi.

"You put it in the suitcase? How are we going to get to it while we're walking?" *Mutti* says, irritated. Unsnapping the lock, she throws out the clothes that Hedi had painstakingly packed, until she finds the bread, and puts it in her purse. Gathering the contents from the floor into her arms, she dumps it back into the suitcase, but now it will not lock.

"Sit on this suitcase," she says brusquely. We sit down and strain to be heavier so the suitcase could be locked. "Bounce down real hard." She clicks the lock shut. "Let's get out of here before the planes come back." She divides our baggage among us to carry, and we hurry out to the street.

Weakened as we are by the lack of food and the constant threat of danger, our progress is painfully slow. Sensing my mother's worry, I carry my burden without complaint, even though flashes of light caused by a deep fatigue dance behind my eyes. My feet move forward by themselves. My cap has slipped off my disheveled hair and the knotted woolen string under my chin loosens with each step. My arms hang down as I drag the packages along the sidewalk. I stagger. I know I cannot give up. My mother and sister need me to do my share, but it is never enough. I feel guilty about my frailties and wish I were stronger. I feel that my weakness is hindering them.

"Hildie, you're dropping your things. Wake up!" My mother sets the luggage down. Hedi leans on the valise, taking deep breaths.

Mutti walks back to retrieve the items I have dropped. She wipes my brow, and we resume walking. She encourages us "Not too much farther. See down that hill by the group of people? That's where we're going."

"Will there be water to drink?" I ask wiping my sweaty brow.

"Yes. You can rest there."

"Thank you," I whisper.

~ ~ ~ ~ ~ ~

*T*he depot is filled with desperate people searching for ways to leave the city before the next air attack. Hearing a locomotive engine chug to life, everybody starts running toward it. Hedi and I run with our mother across railroad ties, over unstable gravel, and around bombed-out craters, to the cattle cars beyond. There we hand our bags to our mother as she throws them onto the car's floor over her head. People jostle, and I am thrown down in the confusion. All I can see are fast-moving legs trampling me. My mother picks me up, heaving me onto the car floor next to Hedi. Hedi shoves me back into the car, holding out her hands to help *Mutti* up.

The floor along the sides of the car is occupied, leaving a little space in the middle, but people keep forcing their way on. Finally, a few young boys and old men stand at the door refusing to let any more on. Baggage and people are thrown helter-skelter together with barely enough room to move. If one person moves, another must get out of the way, making another person move. There is no space to sit. I turn my head from side to side, trying to comprehend what to do in the midst of the boiling chaos all around. Frightened that I am separated from my family, I scream, "*Mutti! Mutti!*"

From somewhere among the moving bodies, I hear my mother's muffled voice, "I'm here, Hildie. Stay where you are. Don't move." Someone moving a large suitcase knocks me down. Afraid of losing my place, I jump up and fiercely push packages aside, trying to plant my feet on the exact spot my mother had told me not to move from. If anyone jostles me, I angrily shove them back with my hands.

"This is my place. Get away," I say, my teeth bared, my eyes filled with rage. I know my duty. It was to keep this spot for my mother. Lugging our largest suitcase, my mother forces her way through the crowd and dumps it at my feet, "Here. Sit on this. Don't let anyone take it. Where is Hedi?" I shake my head. My eyes search the turmoil, afraid that I had not done my part well because I had lost Hedi.

"Hedi, Hedi," my mother calls anxiously.

"Here, *Mutti*," comes a reply in a voice stripped of its vitality.

"Where are you?" calls *Mutti*.

"Over here. I have a suitcase," answers Hedi from a deep corner. My mother grabs people, shoves them down, and steps on baggage until she finds Hedi, glowering at Bertha, the heavy-set woman from the apartment, who was now sitting on one of our suitcases.

"That's our suitcase, but she won't give it to me," says Hedi. When Bertha sees our mother, she gets up without a word. Giving the woman a deadly look, *Mutti* grabs the suitcase.

"Follow me, Hedi." Fighting their way through the crowd, she lays the suitcase next to the one I am guarding. "Sit on this. Don't either of you move," she says, plunging back into the turmoil.

"Quick. Put your legs on my suitcase. I see another piece of our things," says Hedi.

"No. *Mutti* said not to move. You can't go."

"Do it. Do you hear me? Do it!" she threatens, her face drawing into an angry mask. I sprawl my body, face down, over both suitcases.

Hedi returns with a small valise. I rearrange my body so I touch it, too. My eyes dart back and forth reassuring myself that each piece assigned to my protection is still there. When my mother appears with another piece, I am sitting on top guarding each piece. If someone brushes against any part, I kick them, screaming, "Get away. This is ours!"

"Here. Hold this in your arms. Whatever you do, don't let this get stolen." Hedi shoves the case with the food into my arms.

"Oh, the food!"

"Shut up. Don't ever say that word again. It had better be here when I get back," says Hedi. I clutch it so tightly to my bosom my arms ache. Suspicious of everyone, I know the gravity of my responsibility to the family's survival. When my mother and sister return, they sit on the suitcases because there is no other space. "We're missing some things," points out Hedi.

"I know. Just forget it. Hildie has what really counts," says our mother. I am relieved when my mother takes the case with the food and valuables from me. One by one, the people settle down. Bodies press against each other. Those by the doorway have no place to sit. Slowly, the people accept the conditions in the train. The struggle to resist the ugliness ceases, and people are relieved just to have a place to sit, or to be able to stretch out one cramped leg. Our mother slips each of us a boiled potato. Those who are fortunate enough to have food eat also. The less fortunate stare with desperate eyes. I am about to share my potato with a small, monkey-faced child. "No!" *Mutti* commands, pulling my hand back. The child crawls back to a heap of baggage.

The train jerks. Loud noises outside get closer. The conductor comes to our car to slide the door shut. Some of the men near the door inside hold the door so it could not shut. The people in the car plead not to close it, but the men outside the car are stronger. They slam the door shut and place a barricade across on the outside, locking us into total darkness.

People scream and pound on the doors. Some fall over others when the speeding train begins to sway. The confined atmosphere is filled with the sounds of hysterical screams, wretched, pain-filled moans, and the stench of vomit and diarrhea. I sit frozen in the horrible smelling blackness.

I feel the agony pulling me into the frozen void again. Hysterical, I scream, "Open the door. I can't breathe. Open the door. I can't breathe!" I plunge toward the door, beating on it with my fists. My mother swings me down with a thud to my place on the suitcases, saying, "Stop it! We're all in here."

The black air is thick with sickness and misery. With each breath I take, the insidious, velvety black evil insinuates itself deeper into every cell of my body.

Then something compels me to look up. High on the right side of the car, I can see a blue rectangle of light. My head snaps back, my eyes stay glued to the blue light. Gone are all sounds, smells, and feelings. My eyes never blink, even when rags soaked in vomit and diarrhea are thrown through the opening, obstructing my view momentarily. My eyes adjust automatically to the fading light, but there came a point when the rectangle blended into the blackness within. "*Mutti*, why is the light gone?"

"What light? There is no light in here," *Mutti* answers groggily.

"Yes. There was, up there, but now it's gone. Look, there."

I shake my mother's arm. "Please! Tell me where the light from up there has gone."

Looking to where I point, she says, "That was daylight; now it's evening. The light will be back in a few hours." Feeling my anxiety, she says, "I promise. The light will be back."

I resume my vigil, waiting for the light to reappear. Frightened that it will not reappear, I am barely able to breathe. I know that if the light does not return, I will give up. Cramped between two suitcases, with a package under my legs, I doze. Awakening with a start, my eyes fly open seeking the rectangle of light.

Just then, the train jerks to a halt, and the barricade on the door is removed from the outside. The door slides open with a bang. "Fifteen minute stop!" a man shouts as he hurries to the next car, shouting the same message. Those who are able leave the cars. Others, too sick to move, gratefully gulp in breaths of fresh air.

The train jerks again. The people from outside climb on board, but no one locks the door this time. The speeding train causes the people to sway dangerously close to the open door where the rush of air chills them. After a loud exchange of words, someone closes the door leaving a crack a foot wide to allow fresh air in.

Once, the train stops for water. A man brings a bucket from which the people fill their cups and containers.

Early the next day, the train stops for hours. We hear heavy bomb-filled planes fly overhead. The people wait inside. Bombs blow up trains on other tracks, but our cattle cars are spared. When the planes leave, the train speeds on for endless hours to another unknown destination.

~ ~ ~ ~ ~ ~

*F*inally, at night, the train comes to a stop in a town. No one stirs in the car. People from the town help move the sick to the second floor of a large hall where three-tiered bunk beds have been crudely nailed together. There is barely enough room to walk between the tiers. In the middle of the room is an empty space where announcements are made, mail is distributed, and meals are served to the refugees. Food is in short supply. A lukewarm, vile, grayish liquid with grease floating on the top is usually served as soup once a day.

Water for drinking and personal hygiene is also scarce. Body and head lice, as well as bed bugs, add lesions to our already unhealthy skin. Hedi's and my cracked skin is covered with painful sores. Too weak and sick to move, most people doze away the dreary days and nights.

Our mother sleeps in the first tier, nearest the floor. Hedi is in the middle tier, and I sleep on the top tier, close to the ceiling. I often whimper because I am afraid of being so high. Looking down makes me dizzy. Envious of the friends my sister has already made, I watch them play among the bunks, and I listen to the mournful songs of Hedi's friend, Anna. "My sister always seems to make friends," I think.

"Hildie, come down and play with Hedi," *Mutti* coaxes.

"No, I'm too tired."

"You ask her to play with you," I hear my mother whisper to Hedi.

Hedi whispers back, "If she wants to play, let her ask or join us. I don't want to take care of her. She doesn't know how to play. She's no fun." Silence.

"Come and play with us," says Hedi to me.

"No."

Hedi whispers to *Mutti*, "There. I asked, and she said no."

Mutti whispers back, "She needs exercise. If spends too much time in bed, she'll get even weaker."

Standing on her bed, Hedi looks into my feverish eyes. "Hildie, I really want you to play with me," she says persuasively. "Really. I'll help you down."

At this, I smile and swing my legs over the wooden slat by my head. Hedi guides my legs to the slat below. My toes barely touch, and Hedi says from below, "Let go. I'll catch you." Loosening my grip from the rough wooden slat, I tumble on top of Hedi.

Pushing me off, Hedi says, "Run. Here comes Gerhardt. He's IT. Don't let him catch you." I run half way around the square in the middle of the room, but my shortness of breath and the sparks of lights shooting across my eyes stop me. Gerhardt tags me, but I am too tired and dizzy to play. I walk to my mother's bed and fall on it to rest.

"Why are you lying down? You're IT. You can't stop now. You're IT," says Hedi.

"I don't want to play. I'm too tired."

"Okay. I'll be IT for you," says Hedi, chasing another small girl. Hedi's gaunt body emphasizes her height, making her seem older than she is.

At night, I doze in a fitful, nightmare-filled sleep. "*Mutti*, turn off the lights," I beg day and night. "Please turn off the lights."

"We have to leave the lights on. It keeps the mice and rats away. And the bed bugs don't like light," answers *Mutti*.

Our mother has complained vehemently to the camp organizers about the food and sanitary conditions. One day, a soldier stands in the square in the middle of the room, saying, "People, fellow countrymen, the war is almost over. Defeat is difficult, but continue to be brave. Remember, we are Germans. Don't complain. Who is Katherine Weiler?"

Our mother steps forward, "I am."

"Your complaints have reached high officials. How can you be unhappy? You have a bed and get fed each day."

"You call that stinking, slimy water food? Look at our children. See how thin and unhealthy they are. They're covered with lice. We have no soap or hot water to wash the sores on their bodies," she complains bitterly.

"We are doing the best we can under the circumstances," he replies, raising his voice.

She raises hers louder. The other refugees listen in silence. *Mutti* continues, "We're overrun with mice and rats and bed bugs. Sick people receive no medical attention. They just lie in a heap of misery, uncared for."

"We can't do more. You are an example of a good German woman. You have the courage to fight for what you believe, but there comes a time when it takes courage to stop complaining and to live in dignity. Germany has done all she can."

"Then get help from the Red Cross. Don't let the children die."

That's enough!" he shouts. "We are Germans. The children will survive." Then in a soft, emotion-laden voice, he says, "Think of our young soldiers, your husbands and sons, dying at the front for us, all alone. Think of how they are suffering." Pushing *Mutti* aside, the people press closer to the soldier and ask questions.

"When will the war be over?" they ask. He shrugs.

"Have we really lost?" they persist. He nods.

A few women cry softly. The soldier glances at *Mutti* as he turns to leave.

The people creep back to their beds, speaking in hushed tones. Anna, who is two years older than Hedi, begins singing songs about homesickness in her beautiful voice. A sadness fills her soft, brown eyes as she stares at the slats supporting the mattress above. Tears flow down her temples into her chestnut-brown hair. Others join her in song. Some just listen to her crystal voice. I hang down over the edge of my bed, listening and watching Anna's face. Softly, I repeat the words to myself, memorizing the tunes and stanzas.

Anna rarely speaks to anyone but Hedi. Somehow she had become separated from her family. She worries about them constantly and often she weeps quietly. I like her gentleness, and share her sorrow, though she and I never speak.

After the incident with the soldier, the other refugees shun our family. Unwilling to remain in this atmosphere, our mother arranges with a farmer to drive us to a nearby city. There we share a tiny apartment with other families. At least we have the privacy of one tiny room.

Here I become very ill. *Mutti* is frantic with worry because she cannot get milk or even an egg for nourishment. My skin turns yellow. My eyelids are coated with a greenish-gray discharge, and I am always in feverish pain. One of the other tenants, an older woman, obtains some milk. *Mutti* pleads with her to give the milk to me. The woman becomes angry, saying that there is nothing wrong with me; all the children are sickly.

"She's very sick. Come look at her. Just look at her yourself. Please," my mother pleads.

Angrily the woman stomps into the room where I lay. When she sees me, she gasps, pulling back. "Take the milk, but it won't help her anymore. It's a waste to give it to her."

My mother boils the milk and feeds it to me, one spoonful at a time. She sponges the dried discharge from my eyes with warm water, placing cool compresses on my forehead. The other tenants share my mother's vigilant care, and slowly my condition improves. My mother credits my recovery to the milk the old woman had given. She thanks her profusely. When I am stronger, my mother makes me offer thanks also.

Chapter Seven

———————————

"*You are very complicated, very sensitive, finely strung,*" *says Dr. Gregg.*

I am surprised by his comment. "Complicated? Me?" I ask.

"Yes, you are complicated. Do you know this about yourself?"

"I don't think so," I answer.

"How does that make you feel?"

"It makes me feel sad. It makes me feel alone. How can I belong? How can I have someone close to me?" I question him. "Do you think it is hard for people to get to know me?"

"With effort a person can get to know you. You are not closed. With trust and patience of another person, you are knowable."

I think about my inner world when I was seven years old, and the ways in which I tried to make sense of the confusion, the destruction, and the chaos around me. What was the meaning of it?

"What are thinking right now?" asks Dr. Gregg.

"I remember the rubble. And being on my own. There was in my mind always the hope that maybe I will find something beautiful. Like a piece of lace. Or a teacup."

~ ~ ~ ~ ~ ~

*A*t last, the bombings cease. One day, the people line both sides of the rubble-filled streets. I stand next to my mother, watching a tank roll ever so slowly down the middle of the street. The gun moves back and forth. The lid is open. A khaki-clad soldier's head and upper torso emerge. His eyes scan the crowd. Unsure of how to react, I pull my mother's coat. "It's okay. They're Americans. They won't hurt you," says *Mutti*.

The soldier's eyes meet mine. I grin, waving shyly. He smiles. Suddenly, my mother shoves my hand down, and I hear the crowd murmur disapproval of my behavior.

"Stop that. You're German," *Mutti* growls.

"But you said we are also American citizens, and...." *Mutti's* hand clamps my mouth shut, and she whispers hotly into my ear, "You are German. Don't say another word until we get home." The crowd watches a page of history ending as the long streams of tanks crunch over the rubble-strewn streets.

At dusk, the crowd disperses, and I question my mother, "You said we're Americans, and that I didn't have to be afraid of Americans. Didn't you?"

I could remember times she had allayed our fears when stories spread about possible retaliation on civilians by the Americans. She had told us that she and *Grossvater* had worked in America and were citizens of the United States. Now she looks at me and says, "Hildie, we were born Germans."

"But we were born in Yugoslavia, now it's Hungary. Are we Serbian or Hungarian? Are we German citizens?"

"Well, not exactly. Hungary says we are citizens of Hungary ."

"But..." I start to question, confused.

"You're German," she says, "and we are in Germany. Don't mention America again. They're the enemy. It's dangerous to say otherwise."

But I know my mother likes Americans by the way she has spoken of them earlier. Yet, her family was German, and they were born in Hungary. It is all very confusing.

The next day, the looting starts and the streets are unsafe. Although we have only a little food, our family stays indoors watching the activities outside from our second-story window with the other tenants. American soldiers, rifles slung over their shoulders, patrol the streets. Arsonists destroy stores.

To me, it is never quite clear if the American soldiers or the German people are responsible for the looting and arson. Our mother frequently leaves Hedi and me to search for food, but food is scarce. Then one day, her face wreathed in smiles, she comes home with tins of meat and crackers. On another day, there is a case of sugar cubes.

After a week, Hedi and I are allowed to go outside. Doors and windows have been ripped away from most stores, their contents dumped on the sidewalk and street. At first, soldiers carrying rifles force the people away, but eventually they just stand by while the people ransack the merchandise.

The mood of the crowds of people is unstable. Sometimes the air is festive when the people snatch food or clothing. At other times, the people show anger, feeling betrayed when they see the large quantities the merchants had been hoarding. The crowds on the verge of rioting vent their hostilities at the soldiers. The air is charged, waiting for a spark to ignite it.

I stroll past the stores with my mother and sister at first, but later I go out by myself, always returning home empty handed. One day, I come upon a dense crowd. Pushing my way through, I find a huge tangled heap of shoes. To the side, in front of the store where the door used to be, a soldier stands, his rifle held across his chest, poised, ready for all eventualities. The people are rummaging through the mismatched shoes, looking for a pair.

I know this is wrong; it is stealing. I stand on the edge of the heap, uncertain what to do. Behind me, two women argue whether or not it is stealing to take things from the ransacked stores. I listen to their debate. One says, "It's wrong to take things that belong to someone else. It's stealing."

"No, it isn't. We didn't break into the store. We didn't throw these shoes onto the sidewalk," says the second woman.

"But if we take them, we'll be just as guilty as those who broke into the store."

"What's right or wrong? We're starving. Our clothes are threadbare and torn. Our shoes don't fit, and they have holes in them. If we don't take what we need, someone else will. Look at this little girl. She's nothing but skin and bones. Look at her shoes; they're obviously too small for her, and the tops are all cracked. She has no shoelaces."

To me she says, "Go on. Get yourself a new pair of shoes." I hesitate, unsure of the validity of this woman's argument. "Go on. It's all right. Take them. No one cares," the woman persists. The other woman scowls.

Seeing a red shoe, I take a step toward it and then stop. The soldier is watching me. I kick the red shoe with my big toe. I think that the cherry-red shoe is the most beautiful thing I have ever seen. I want it so much that my chest aches. Shyly I look at the soldier sideways. He nods approval. In an instant, I snatch the shoe, and run home, clutching the prize to my breast.

"Well, you finally brought something home," *Mutti* says approvingly.

My eyes shining, I proudly show her the poppy-red shoe. "That's a very bright color. Do they fit? Let's see," says my mother, slipping the shoe on my foot. "Your socks have more holes than material. Tonight I'll mend them for you. They'll be as good as new. Well, the shoe is a little too big. Didn't you try it on first?" I shake my head. "I'll stuff some paper into the toes, and you'll be able to wear them. Give me the other shoe. I'll fix them both for you."

"I don't have it. Just this one."

"What? What good is one shoe? It takes two shoes to make a pair, just like your feet—two to make a set."

"But this shoe is brand new, and it's such a pretty color," I say while tenderly stroking the smooth leather.

"Go back and find the other shoe. Make sure they're the same size."

"Oh, no. I can't go back. *Mutti*, please, I can't. It isn't right."

"One shoe is useless. You might as well throw it out."

Looking at the shoe, I know my mother is right. My eyes plead with her.

But *Mutti* is firm. "No. I won't go with you. I have been out all day looking for food. I'm tired. You're old enough to know that one shoe is useless," she shakes her head disapprovingly. "When are you going to learn to take care of yourself? Your sister and I do everything for you. And now you come home with one useless shoe. Throw it out. I don't want to look at it anymore," says *Mutti*, lying down wearily on the bed to rest.

The truth of her words hurts. I decide to look for the other shoe so *Mutti* will be happier. Anyway, I have to have the mate because I've never seen shoes of such a beautiful color.

Holding the shoe, I stand in front of the heap of shoes still being picked through by the scavengers. As hard as I try, I cannot join them without permission. I walk over to the soldier and say, "I have only one shoe. I need the other one. May I look for it?" He just looks at me. I said, louder, "May I look for the other shoe?" I notice the people on top of the heap standing motionless watching the two of us.

The soldier glances nervously around, and then looks at me. I hold up the one red shoe high enough for him to see, "I need the other shoe." Still silent, he nods. His face is flushed, and he shuffles his feet, repositioning his rifle. The soldier watches as I kneel to sort through the huge pile of shoes. After what seems like hours of sorting, I still have not found the mate. I look toward the soldier. He rolls his eyes and head toward the right, moving, and kicking a red shoe. Elated, I pick it up. But it is much too big. Near tears, I look at the soldier again.

It is dusk. I try one last desperate time to find the mate. Most people are gone by now. I sit in the middle of the pile, the soldier watching. I sort through a few more shoes, but the fading light makes it difficult to see. I stand up, and throw my one red shoe onto the heap. Heading for home, I wipe tears from my eyes.

The soldier watches me walk alone on the sidewalk as he continues his solitary vigil. I hate going home empty-handed. I know my mother will still be angry with me. In my heart, I know that I am not doing my share to stay alive. I try so hard. I seldom cry now. I never ask for food. I never complain of being cold anymore. I never tell anyone how dizzy I feel sometimes, or how often everything gets black when I move, or how tiny sparks dance before my eyes, or how much my head or chest hurts, or how often I cannot catch my breath. I know I should be doing more, but I do not know what else.

When I get home *Mutti* asks, "Did you find the other shoe?"

"No," I shake my head dejectedly.

"I told you to go back and look for it. Why didn't you go back?"

"I did. It wasn't there."

"Well, it had to be there. Who would take just one shoe? You didn't look, did you?"

"Yes, I did. The soldier helped me look too, but they didn't fit or maybe I got mixed up. I don't know."

"The soldier helped you? The one with the rifle helped you?" my mother asks, incredulous. "Yes. I asked him if I could look for the mate." I rattle on, telling my mother all the details of my search.

My mother's face softens. "It's okay. When the war is over, I'll buy you the prettiest red shoes you've ever seen."

Disbelieving, I look at my mother. "I promise," she says. "Anyway, your shoes are fine for now. I found some shoe polish that will make them shine like a mirror, and these shoelaces will make them feel more comfortable. Red shoes are fine for ballerinas, but not here, not now; they would get too dusty."

~ ~ ~ ~ ~ ~

Now the war is definitely over for Germany. The deadly rain of bombs has ceased, bringing a degree of regularity to our family. Each night we sleep in the same apartment, knowing that the next night we will sleep in the same bed. The worry of feeding the three of us continues to plague our mother, who spends her days in the endless pursuit of keeping her family alive. Being preoccupied with survival, she continues to allow Hedi and me great freedom to roam and explore. Although warned by my mother to stay out of bombed-out buildings and to keep away from the heaps of rubble, I pay no attention. A force greater than my mother's warning seems to draw me to the forbidden spaces. Each morning, regardless of the weather, I eagerly look forward to my wanderings.

"Good-bye," I call, sliding my coat off the hook on the wall.

"Going out again? Stay away from the mounds of rubble. You're not going into bombed buildings, are you?" *Mutti* questions.

"No." I turn to avoid my mother's eyes.

"Hildie, turn around. Look at me. Are you going through bombed buildings?"

"Everybody searches through the rubble. I'm not alone. I like trying to figure out what a piece used to be before it was bombed. Sometimes in the midst of broken bricks and scraps of wood, I find things unbroken. Yesterday I found a teacup. It has no cracks, not even a scratch. It has beautiful pink flowers and a real gold handle."

"Why didn't you bring it home? It would be nice to drink out of china again."

"I gave it away. I thought you'd be angry if I told you where I found it."

"Well, I don't want you on those mounds, but a china teacup would have been nice." Pause. "Promise you'll stay away from the mounds? They're unsafe. People get hurt every day by cave-ins. Sometimes tons of bricks are supported by weak timber slats and the added weight makes them collapse."

"I'm not heavy. I'm very careful where I step." I don't tell my mother that I know about the holes under the rubble. That was where I found the teacup. When I go out, I search every crevice, looking for bodies. I keep thinking someone might still be alive. Maybe I can help.

Dark clouds begin to appear in *Mutti's* eyes, "I don't want you on those mounds."

By now, my coat is on. My hand is on the door handle. Looking into *Mutti's* eyes, I say, "I promise. I won't go there today."

In a flash, I let myself out of the apartment, running down the stairs. Halfway down, I stop, clutching the handrail and wall to keep from falling. Suddenly my head aches and everything turns black. I sit on the stairs, still clutching the handrail, forcing myself not to give in to the dizziness.

"I'll be all right," I whisper to myself. "I'll be fine. I just have to rest a while." My head still throbbing. Gingerly, I pull myself down one stair at a time, dreading the moment when I have to stand up. When I reach the bottom of the stairs, I take deep breaths and then stand. Steadying myself against the wall, I wait for the hallway to stop spinning and the pain in my head to subside.

The fresh air revives me. The throbbing of my head lessens. Slowly I walk past several mounds. One had caved in during the night. Around the perimeter, adults and children discuss the dangers they had fortunately escaped by not standing on top when it collapsed. Barely able to control my curiosity to find out what the hole looked like, I remember my promise to *Mutti* and keep on walking.

Like a magnet, I am drawn to my favorite pastime, exploring a row of partially bombed-out buildings. I have often stood in the debris-strewn courtyard, studying the scene. An immense destructive force has ripped the walls away, exposing three apartments, one on top of the other. Metal rods, white crumbling plaster, and splintered wood sag at the edges of each floor. On the top floor, daylight shines through the jagged, broken windowpanes and roofless ceiling, revealing part of a room containing a couch and a floor lamp, waiting for the families to return.

The darkness of the first and second floors frightens me. I imagine something sinister crouching behind the dim outlines of the couches on those floors. I sit on a smooth, broken piece of concrete, carefully brushing off the plaster dust and dirt. I know my mother will be angry if I get my clothes dirty. Elbows on my knees, I cup my chin with my hands, continuing to stare. To the left of the couches stands a strangely twisted staircase, loose stairs dangling in the sunlight. I have been able to explore the other partially destroyed buildings, but this, my favorite, appears inaccessible. I ache to sit on the sunlit couch on the third floor, to feel a part of the happy normal life I imagine has taken place there. Here I find a bittersweet peace.

Hours pass. Unable to figure out how I can safely sit on that couch, I decide to visit my second favorite spot, a few blocks closer to home. Taking one last look at the beckoning couch, I skip down the street until the pain in my head becomes unbearable and I feel weak. I slow down, pressing my temples to stop the throbbing. Then rigidly erect, I walk on. I am hungry, but I know there is no food at home. "Better to explore," I think.

When I arrive at my destination, I look around making sure no one is watching me. I duck down, crawling through a small opening of the bombed building. Inside, I get up, brushing myself off. Taking a deep breath to control my fears, I wait while my eyes adjust to the dimness. The shell of the outer brick walls and part of the roof remain, while the contents of the building lay in a heap inside. The surrounding walls have tall Gothic windows. I love the shapes of the many windows. They feel holy to me, especially on this day, when the sun shines, outlining each shape against the dark walls.

Today, I do not rummage through the debris as usual. I walk to a large, mysterious, cylinder topped with a cone-shaped object, which is partially buried in the ground. The sunlight glistens on the shiny metallic surface near the ground. My hand glides through the arrows of light. As often as I have studied this object, I still cannot decide what it is. I circle it, running my hand across the smooth surface. I step back, studying it in fascination. The object is tightly buried in the ground. I kick it. I stay a long time, pondering. When I tire of the effort to understand, I look to the cathedral-like windows for reassurance.

I notice the afternoon sunlight fading, which means that it is time to go home. One last time, I lay my face on the smooth surface of the strange object. The cool metal feels good on my brow and temples.

That evening for dinner, *Mutti*, Hedi, and I have our usual boiled potatoes and a few of the remaining sugar cubes.

"Did you stay away from the mounds and bombed buildings as I told you?" asks *Mutti*.

"I didn't go on any mounds."

"Did you see the one that caved in? It has a great big hole at the top." Our eyes meet.

"No, *Mutti*, I didn't go near any mounds today," I say.

"And buildings?"

Silence.

"Hildie, did you go to bombed buildings? Answer me. A blond-haired girl was seen on Friederichstrasse entering a building. Was that you? Tell me."

"I only went to two. I'm fine. See?" I raised my arms to show her. "I'm fine. I'm very careful. Please don't be angry. Please."

"Those buildings are ready to collapse at any moment. Buildings are collapsing daily. Last week a child got killed. Stay away."

"I'm careful. I won't get hurt."

"If the buildings don't collapse, there is the danger of rats. They're hungry. They're huge—the size of cats—and they bite children."

"I never see rats."

Hedi interjects, "When you see them, it's too late. If you hear them squeak, you better make a lot of noise and run."

That night, I sleep fitfully. I dream that my favorite buildings have collapsed, and that mammoth rats are attacking me.

For a few days, I heed the warnings, walking nervously up and down the streets, barely noticing the mounds and the people sorting through the rubble. My stomach is in knots. When people speak to me, I seem to have difficulty comprehending. I slip in and out of the frozen void that I had first experienced in Vienna.

Mutti notices my detachment and asks, "What's the matter with you?" I wring my hands and mumble, "I'm fine, I'm fine." I stay in our room most of the time, pacing back and forth. Despite the fear of my mother's anger, the danger of the unsupported walls, and the fierce rats—who at this point in my imagination have huge, bared, razor-sharp teeth—the pull of the couch, the Gothic windows, and the mysterious cone-shaped object is stronger. My journeys to the two buildings resume.

One day, standing in the courtyard staring at the couch on the third floor, I make up my mind. No matter what happens, I know I have to sit on that couch. Shifting from one foot to the other, I look for a possible route. I never sit on the concrete slab anymore because of my fear of rats. I have not seen any, but the squeaks increase daily, and often I hear unexplained rustlings.

I kick a brick. It rolls over, and underneath I find a neatly folded, delicate, white lace handkerchief. Quickly, I stuff it into my pocket. I decide that the only way I can climb up to the couch is by using the rickety staircase. I know I will have to be very careful not to shake it—especially in the middle, where I will have to take a giant step across three stairs that dangle almost free on one side, still barely attached by curving nails. I see another dangerous spot in the gap between the top of the stairs and the third floor. I am sure that if I jump with all my might, I can cover the distance between. Then I will sink into the soft cushions of the couch.

I stand at the foot of the sunlit staircase, looking up. I hear rustling, and wait for it to stop or to be attacked. The rustling stops. I place my left foot on the first rung. Someone shouts. I whirl around and see a soldier in the darkness. He speaks loudly in a language I do not understand. As he comes toward me, my heart skips from fear. Scuttling through the dark opening, I run toward home.

In front of the building with Gothic windows, I crawl through the dark, narrow crevice. The sunlit cathedral windows calm my jangled nerves and jagged breathing. Behind me stands the metallic cone. The solid, ever-present sentinel comforts me, but the squeaks keep me on guard. I face the cone. I have ceased to wonder about its purpose. I have accepted it simply as a constant in my life, never comprehending its potential danger to me, or to the people who live nearby.

As I continue staring, a soldier slowly slides into my view, several steps behind the cone. He speaks softly, lifting up both palms of his hands into the air. He takes a step toward me. I step back. He stops. Our eyes meet. My eyes shyly question. He speaks again softly, calmly, taking another step toward me. I turn around and run, but before sliding through the crevice, I look back at the soldier. He shrugs his shoulders at me, walking around the cone, and writing into a little notebook.

At home, I am quiet and listless. I know I will never return to my buildings. My fears of the rats and of the buildings collapsing are dangers I can cope with, but, men—soldiers—are beyond my abilities. I am too afraid of soldiers because I believe that they were the cause of all the destruction.

The next day, *Mutti* storms into the room, "We have to leave early tomorrow morning and be gone all day. The soldiers found an unexploded bomb half-buried in the old church near here. Hildie, I know you used to go in there. Didn't you see it?"

"A bomb? No. What's it look like?"

"I don't know. Let's go visit the Kramers. From their porch on the third floor, you can see the bombed building where it is."

The three of us walk to the Kramer's porch, where people are running up and down the stairs, talking excitedly, and looking down. I look down at the milling crowd near my mysterious cone shaped object. I think how different it looks from this angle. The ring of earth around it is more pronounced than I remember it from the ground. Soldiers shoo the people away. Mothers are calling their children home.

"Where's the bomb, *Mutti*?" I ask.

"Right there, in front of you. Can't you see it?"

"You're afraid of that?" I laugh. "It won't hurt you. I play with it all the time."

The people who overhear gasp, "You played with the bomb?"

"That's the bomb?" I ask, unbelieving. "Are you sure? It's so smooth and cool. Are you sure it's a bomb?"

"Yes. That's why we're being evacuated tomorrow. The soldiers are going to detonate it, but it might explode by accident."

"Are you sure?"

"Yes. The soldiers know a bomb when they see it. It's one of theirs," *Frau* Kramer says contemptuously. "They dropped it on us," her eyes glittering with hatred.

Early the next morning, army vans drive the neighborhood residents to a large meadow. A few hours later, we are able to return home.

I like to play with the lace handkerchief I found near the staircase. I place it on the table, smoothing out the wrinkles, tracing the delicate intricate design with my fingertips. Hedi touches the fragile, fluted edges. We share a rare moment of tenderness.

"It looks like a spider's web," says Hedi, softly.

"Where did you get that handkerchief?" asks *Mutti*.

"I found it," I answer.

"Where?"

"Outside. Under a brick."

Mutti sighs. She looks troubled and seems lost in thought for several minutes. Finally, she declares, "We have to get out of here. It's too dangerous. There are probably other unexploded bombs. They don't have enough equipment to raze the damaged buildings." She pauses again, then goes on, "We don't belong here. They don't really consider us Germans. You're both becoming like uneducated, wild street urchins. And, food is still such a problem. There is no hope for a better life here."

"Where do you think we should go next? Where would we have more food?" asks Hedi, sympathetic to *Mutti*'s feelings.

"I don't know. I guess we should go home. Your grandparents may still be in Miletisch, or at least I might be able to find out where they are." She pauses again. "Here we have nothing."

Then, as she had often done during our journey, *Mutti* searches through our belongings for the roll of needlepoint canvases Hedi had stuffed into a valise when we left home. She unrolls the canvases on the table. Gently running her fingertips over the many hued intricate designs, she seems to remember our earlier life where beauty could be expressed. We three become engrossed in the largest needlepoint, the one that had poppy-red, vibrant pink, and regal lavender carnations artistically arranged in a periwinkle-blue vase. A plate of grapes, apples, and pears spilled across the pink tablecloth in the foreground of the canvas.

"Remember the shop where we selected the threads?" *Mutti* muses, recalling for us our former life. Together, we look at all the needlepoint scenes — the ancient white Greek-columned buildings surrounded by autumn trees, the plumed bird and muted colored flowers against a robin's-egg-blue background. My favorite is a graceful, steepled, fairytale castle nestled high on green rolling hills with brown hedges winding downward to an azure blue sea. I am reminded of home by a tiny, slanted, red roofed house near a flower-strewn stream.

Finally, *Mutti* looks up from the needlepoint scenes. "It's time to go home," she says. "May Gold help us."

Part III

After the War
Hope for a Better Life

Chapter Eight

"When the war was over, did you go home?" asks Dr. Gregg.

"No, we couldn't."

"Why not?"

"I still don't really understand," I tell Dr. Gregg, wearily. I am exhausted from the weeks of recalling my childhood experiences. I continue, to try to explain to him, "The political borders had changed, and we were not allowed to go back to our home."

"Tell me about it," he says. "As best you can."

"I don't know," I say. "Even now, the question continues to haunt me: Why were those with German last names imprisoned?"

He waits as I struggle again to make sense of this part of my own story. "The Germans were dragged from their homes and placed in camps in other towns: Kruschiwel, Gakowa, Karawukowa, Filipowa, Hodschag — and others I don't even know about. I've read that some of the people who survived the camps believe that the Serbian partisans were afraid of an uprising. But, afraid of defenseless old men, women, and children? That doesn't make sense. I've also read that others believed the partisans wanted the Germans ousted so they could resettle their own people into the vacant homes."

I do not understand all the reasons. But, as I sit in Dr. Gregg's office, it is clear to me now that there is no distinction between the soldier who drops the bombs, wreaking havoc below, and the soldier below who loads weapons to destroy the bomber above. Both have to harden themselves against the gentleness of their souls, where goodness resides. Both unleash unspeakable harm to all of humanity, *including themselves, by the violence which acts against a natural respect for life.*

I vividly remember the terrifying descriptions of the suffering in the towns. . . .

~ ~ ~ ~ ~ ~

We travel from Germany back to Hungary. From Bacsalmas, Hungary, we are unable to continue to Miletitsch, the home of my grandparents, because it has become part of Yugoslavia. The borders have been closed, and we cannot return. We are destitute. The Hungarians share what little they have. For a while, we stay with an older couple, who are the parents of my mother's friend. My mother works in the vineyards in the daytime. During the evening, she knits intricately designed sweaters and jumpsuits for babies. This work is in exchange for food and housing. Sitting close to a kerosene lamp, she works late into the night. My sister Hedi tends a cow for a neighbor who in turn gives her lunch and dinner.

"Do I have to take that cow to the meadow?" protests Hedi. "I'm not a cow-herder. That's for poor people, and people who are uneducated."

"I know. It's hard for you" agrees *Mutti*. "You weren't raised to be a cow-herder, but now we are very poor. It's the only way we can get food. Please do it. Swallow your pride. And don't hit the cow with the stick in anger. Stop muttering nasty things under your breath in the street when you walk her. The owner doesn't like it."

"How long will I have to do it?"

"I don't know. I found out that your grandparents are still in Miletitsch. If they send us money or food, you can stop herding the cow."

"School starts tomorrow," says Hedi. "Who will take the cow when I'm in school?"

"You can't go to school. I can't feed you."

"I always go to school. I like school. I like making friends and I get good grades."

"I'll talk to the farmer and see what we can work out, but don't get your hopes up. How are your hands? Let me see them."

Hedi holds out her cracked palms. The cracks are so deep that they often bleed. "They don't seem to be getting better," says *Mutti*. "Take off your dress so I can check the other sores." Gently she turns Hedi around, examining the painful skin eruptions. When she has finished with Hedi, she also examines my diseased skin.

"Are you washing with soap?"

"Yes, but it hurts," replies Hedi.

"I know. I just don't know what else to do."

Just then the older woman enters the room. "Oh, I'm sorry. I didn't know you were bathing the girls."

"Please, come in. Look at my daughters. Have you ever seen anything like this?" The two women examined each of us in turn.

"Oh, my, that looks painful. I've never seen such sores before. They're all over their bodies. Have they had them a long time?" asks the older woman.

"For months. Sometimes the sores clear up and heal, but this time, they don't seem to be getting better. I don't know what to do. Don't you have any ointment? Anything?"

"I have some sulfur ointment, but I don't know if it's good for them. Let me show it to you." We shiver without our clothes while she goes to retrieve it.

The older woman returns carrying a large tin. *Mutti* opens the tin, sniffing the greenish ointment. "It smells awful. Do you think this will help?"

"I don't know. It is to be used on the skin. I've used it, and it helped. Of course, I just used it for insect bites. You're welcome to use it, if you think it will help."

"Let's put it on your hands first," says *Mutti*. When the ointment touches our skin, we both scream, "Stop! Stop! It hurts too much."

"I'm sorry. I know it hurts, but I have to do this. Be brave. Don't cry. This will disinfect the sores and kill the germs," says *Mutti*. We try to stop crying, swallowing hard while she gently smears the ointment on.

The next morning, our mother awakens Hedi and says, "If you still want to go to school, you may go. The farmer agreed to let you take the cow out right after school, and all day Saturday and Sunday. "Are you sure you want to go to school? You know it will be taught in Hungarian. I know you speak Hungarian, but you haven't read or written in Hungarian for quite some time."

"Yes. I want to go. I'll learn. I catch on fast. The other kids will help me. Thank you, *Mutti*." says Hedi. Excitedly, Hedi puts on the clean dress *Mutti* has washed and ironed. She combs her hair carefully and braids it in two faded, tattered red ribbons.

"When you're ready, you may leave. Hildie can't speak Hungarian very well yet, so I'm not sending her to school," *Mutti* says. Hedi skips happily out of the house.

But when she comes home for lunch, she is crestfallen and withdrawn.

"What's the matter, Hedi?" asks our mother.

"Nothing."

"How was school?" No answer. "What happened at school? Don't you like the children?"

"They ... they," she holds back a strangled sob. "They won't play with me because of my hands. They're afraid they might catch it. And, and... and...."

"Yes. And, what?"

"And they wouldn't even let me hold a book. The teacher sat a boy and a girl on either side of me, holding the book in front of me, turning the pages for me."

"See, Hedi," I say, "I told you they would be mean. I told you not to go to school. They don't like you."

"They do too like me. Well, they will like me, once they get to know me. But these hands are ugly. *Mutti*, can they catch it from me?"

"I don't know. Let's bandage your hands. Your dress covers up most of your sores," says *Mutti*. After she finishes bandaging Hedi's hands, *Mutti* reminds her, "Don't forget the cow after school."

~ ~ ~ ~ ~ ~

$\mathcal{A}$ few days later, a fat man and woman pull up with their wagon to deliver packages from Miletitsch to my family. Hedi and I eagerly help our mother open the containers filled with food, coffee, tobacco, and chocolate sent to us by our grandparents. We are excited to see the cooked chickens preserved in lard, and a jar of whole hard boiled eggs floating in spicy vinegar.

"Well, Hedi, your cow-herding days are over. I have enough here to last quite a while on the black market," says *Mutti*.

"Good. Then I can play after school."

"First you come home to do your chores. You may have to take care of Hildie. Selling things on the black market takes lots of time and I may be away for long periods of time. Mr. and Mrs. Brapt have a vineyard across the border. They can get messages to my parents. What a godsend!"

A few days later, a group of children bang on the door to get our mother. "Hurry! Hurry! Hedi's hurt. She needs you," they shout.

"What's the matter with her?"

"We were playing on the old, torn-up railroad tracks. Hedi climbed on the heap of old tracks, and fell. Hurry!"

"Hildie, stay here," *Mutti* says, running out of the house and following the children. Afraid, I pace back and forth biting my nails. I slip in and out of the frozen void. Out of fear, I seem to forget to breathe. Then I force myself to breathe, to be calm.

Finally they return. A man carries Hedi into the house and gently places her on the bed. Her pale face, clothes, and legs are covered with blood. Children and adults mill around while our mother and the man assess Hedi's injuries. Then as I watch, Hedi lets go of the hand she had been squeezing. Thick red blood pumps from her palm.

"We have to stop the bleeding. Give me a clean handkerchief and hurry," says the man. He wads the cloth and applies pressure to the wound.

Mutti scolds Hedi, "What were you doing on those tracks? You know you're not supposed to go there. I told you it's too dangerous."

"All the kids were there. I wasn't alone," answers Hedi.

"I'll bet you were showing off. Why do you always have to climb the highest and run the fastest?"

The man looks into *Mutti*'s worried eyes. "Has the bleeding stopped?" she asks.

"Not completely, but it's easing up. Hold this cloth. Apply enough pressure to stop the bleeding, while I check the rest of her body."

"Are you a doctor?" asks our mother.

"No. There is no doctor in this town."

My mother's eyes waver.

The man says, "I know how to check for cuts and broken limbs. You're upset. She's your daughter. I understand." Pause. "May I check her?"

"Yes. I guess so, if there is no doctor."

Hedi has no other injuries. Two days later, she returns to school with a bulky bandage and a sling for the injured hand. The deep cracks on the other palm showed signs of healing. To Hedi's delight, her classmates give her a heroine's welcome.

A few days later, Hedi collapses at school. At home our mother discovers a huge boil in my sister's armpit. She applies hot compresses day and night. After the boil breaks open, Hedi's fever subsides. She is able to rest a little better, but she is still very ill.

~ ~ ~ ~ ~ ~

*I*n the midst of this intensive caring for Hedi, Mr. and Mrs. Brapt arrive with news from Miletitsch. "Hildie, come in here. Mr. and Mrs. Brapt have news from your grandparents. It's about you," my mother calls.

"Me?" I asked, sitting on the kitchen chair.

"Your grandfather wants us to bring you to Miletitsch," says Mrs. Brapt.

"When do we leave? To Miletitsch? Not to Zombor?" I am happy.

"You'll leave tonight. Hedi and I will follow you later," says my mother.

"I'm going alone?" I ask. My mother nods.

"You're sending me away all by myself?" I am horrified.

"Yes, but we'll come later," reassures my mother.

I throw myself into my mother's arms. "Please, don't make me go," I wail. "I don't want to go without you."

Mutti rocks me, stroking my hair away from my tear‑stained face. "Oh, child. You have to be strong. We've been here two months. We're poor. I can hardly feed you. All of us are sick. You're so thin and sad. *Grossmutter* will cook you chicken soup and dumplings. She's a wonderful cook. You remember her, don't you?" she asks.

I nod, listening, my head against my mother's breast.

"*Grossvater* will protect you. You'll be safe. It's just a little vacation. You remember. You used to go to Miletitsch by yourself before the war.

"I always missed you. If Hedi can stay, why can't I? Or send her away first."

"Hedi is too weak. She'll come when she's stronger. These kind people were sent by *Grossvater* to bring you to Miletitsch. You have to go with them tonight."

"No. I can't. I won't. Please, don't make me," I sob. My irregular breaths make me choke. My mother and I cling to each other.

"Be my good little girl. Do this for me. Be brave. Be strong. No more tears," says my mother. We sit a long time. *Mutti* holds me on her lap while the Brapts look on.

"Please leave us while I dress her," says my mother to the couple.

My mother bathes me. Around my midriff, she ties a pink satin money belt and instructs me, "Don't take this belt off until you are with *Grossvater*." She holds my head with both hands, looking into my eyes, saying, "Remember, don't take it off. If you get into trouble, use it. You won't need it, because you'll be safe. Give it to *Grossvater*. You'll be safe."

When she finishes dressing me, my mother takes my eight-year-old-hand, and walks outside to the couple, and says, "She's ready. I've packed a small overnight bag as you told me. Take good care of her. My father will reward you well. I'm sure he has already given you a generous advance."

"Yes, but we aren't doing this for the money. We want to help you," says the woman.

"I thank you for your kindness. My father will reward you. No harm must come to her. You know my father, so you know he's strong. His family is very important to him," says my mother. She knows that these people have never had more than a small vineyard, which is now located in Yugoslavia. Their need is the only guarantee of her daughter's safety.

My mother kneels in front of me, embracing and kissing me. I start to cry. "Don't cry. I want you to promise you won't cry anymore. Promise." I swallow hard, nodding. "Be strong. Be brave. Kiss my *Mutter* and *Vater*. Hedi and I will follow soon. Don't cry. You'll be safe. Do what Mr. and Mrs. Brapt tell you. Tomorrow you'll see Theresa and Nicky and your grandparents."

She places me on the back of the wagon. The horses clomp down the street, pulling the wagon in the darkness. I sit motionless, watching my mother fade out of sight. After a while, the swaying of the wagon rocks me into a merciful sleep.

When the wagon stops in front of a house, Mrs. Brapt quickly bundles me inside so that neighbors would not see me. "Sit down on this chair," says Mrs. Brapt, groping around in the darkness for the kerosene lamp. The lighted lamp casts strange shadows on the wall. I watch the couple preparing a simple supper of grapes and bread.

"Pull your chair up and eat," says Mr. Brapt.

"Thank you, but I'm not hungry."

"You have to eat. You'll get sick. Eat some of this bread."

"No, thank you," I shove the bread back to Mr. Brapt.

"Get your nightgown on and get some sleep. We'll get up early in the morning. You'll sleep on the couch over there. My wife and I'll sleep over in our big bed in the corner."

"Is this your bedroom?" I ask.

"Yes. It's our bedroom, our kitchen, our only room. It's small; but it's ours, all ours. Come, I'll help you get ready for bed. What do you see behind me that you're staring at?" asks Mrs. Brapt.

"The shadows are moving."

"When we're in bed, we'll put out the lamp and they'll go away." The woman's fat clumsy hands pull my dress over my head.

"Take off your undershirt," says Mrs. Brapt.

"No. I'll leave it on," I say.

"Take it off." When I hesitate, the woman says, "Your mother told you to obey us. Now take it off." I took off the last piece of clothing, standing naked in the dim light.

"What's that around your waist?" asks the man, his heavy body straddling the chair, soiled rumpled trousers covering his legs.

"It's a belt," I answer.

"Take it off. Let me see it," says Mrs. Brapt sweetly.

"No. *Mutti* said not to let anyone touch it."

"You can't sleep with it on. It will keep you awake. Let me hold it for you overnight," says Mrs. Brapt.

I place my hands on the pink satin to protect it.

"Didn't your mother tell you to obey us?" asks Mr. Brapt.

"Yes."

"Then give me that belt," says Mr. Brapt.

I am confused. I try to remember all the things my mother had told me, but I had been too upset. I recall my mother telling me to obey these strangers. But to give them the money belt does not seem right. I step back.

"No. You can't have it," I say, my voice shaking.

"I've never seen a belt like that. I want to see it," says Mr. Brapt, stepping toward me.

"You leave me alone! This belt is for my *Grossvater* Westermeyer. If you touch me, he'll be mad at you. He won't like it that you treated me like this," my voice cracks. I am near tears, despite my promise to my mother.

At the mention of the Westermeyer name, Mr. Brapt stops. The couple exchange glances. Returning to the chair, he continues eating. "Put your nightgown on. You'll catch a chill. Wipe your face with this wet cloth," says Mrs. Brapt. I wipe my face and lay on the couch.

Placing the cover over me, Mrs. Brapt says, "We're nice to you. We meant no harm. You misunderstood. We just wanted you to be comfortable. You don't have to tell your *Grossvater* about this. You're just tired." I do not answer, clutching the satiny belt under my nightgown.

The Brapts time their journey so we will arrive at the border at mid-morning, when the traffic is the heaviest. They count on the border guards being too busy to notice a small child being smuggled across.

As the border comes into sight, Mrs. Brapt says to me, "Come up front. Sit down between us. Make yourself as little as possible. When the guard checks us, look cheerful, but don't say anything. Oh, no, your blonde hair has to be covered. They'll know you're German. Let me tie my scarf on your head." Mrs. Brapt makes a wide fold across my forehead. Making sure to conceal every strand of hair, she ties the brightly flowered scarf under my chin. "She has blue eyes! Oh, no, she has blue eyes," says Mrs. Brapt.

"It's too late now. Hildie, don't look into the guard's eyes. Keep your eyes downcast," says Mr. Brapt.

To his wife he said, "Stop worrying. Joke with the guards. Be relaxed. Act like it's just another day's work in the vineyard."

When the wagon in front pulls away, the guard walks over to the Brapt wagon. "Another day's work, eh? You're a little late, aren't you?" the guard asks, poking around the parcels on the back of the wagon.

"The woman overslept. You know how they are," grumbles Mr. Brapt.

"Well, what have we here? Is this little girl going along to help you?" asks the guard.

I can no longer contain my curiosity. I look into the guard's eyes, smiling. "A nice little girl. Nice blue eyes," says the guard. He speaks to me in a language I do not understand. In Hungarian, he asks,

"What's your name, little girl?" As I open my mouth to answer, Mrs. Brapt sharply kicks me, hard, with her toe. The horses' impatience causes the wagon to move sharply.

"Go ahead. Keep moving. See you tonight. Don't work too hard," says the guard, motioning them along.

Hours later, the wagon pulls through the Westermeyer's huge gate.

"Oh, my poor child," exclaims *Grossmutter*, seeing my thinness and unhealthy pallor. My grandfather pays the Brapts immediately, and they hurry to cross the border back into Hungary.

Chapter Nine

"*May I tell you a story?*" I ask Dr. Gregg. "*I often tell stories, which probably take much too long, but I think this is very important.*"

"*Yes, I love stories,*" he replies eagerly.

"*When my mother died, I was 30 years old. Her death was very hard for me. I had such deep fears of dying and being separated from my mother. Before our relatives closed her coffin, I insisted on having the cross that was inside near her head. This caused quite a stir in my Catholic family. How could they possibly bury her without that cross...it was a sacrilege, they argued. Through the commotion, I heard a voice saying, 'Give her the cross, the flowers in her coffin are in the shape of the cross.' And so, they gave it to me.*"

Staring off into space, I am lost in my thoughts. I don't know how long I am in this state.

"*Oh, let's see now, where was I? Oh, yes. I loved my mother dearly. So this simple brass cross has hung on a wall in my bedroom close to 20 years. But, last week, I took the cross off the wall and gave it away.*"

"*What do you think this means to you?*"

"*Yes, that is the question, isn't it? I think that I have now released her. Accepted her death. Probably there are many other levels, but I have a sense of peace and joy in the act of giving the cross away.*"

"*How did your mother die? Was she ill?*"

"*She had breast cancer that became lung cancer. She was very ill for over four years. She moved in with me, my husband, and two* small children. I took care of her for about nine months. It was exhausting. She was so brave and courageous, both during the war and throughout her illness."

"How was that?"

"It's hard to know all the levels of her heart the last few months of her life. She never complained. She so regretted that I had to care for her at my young age. She wanted to talk to me about her dying, to prepare me, but I couldn't and just kept repeating that she'll recover. Of course, we both knew that this wasn't true because my sister and I had told her months earlier that the cancer was terminal. She read and reread the 23rd Psalm."

"And now?" he asks.

"And now, I can finally release her. Why now after so many, many years?" I ask him.

"It's hard to know. Some things simply have their own time," he answers.

"Part of it is that it's probably the first time in my entire life that I am able to talk with another person about the things that have been locked so deeply in my heart…it's healing."

~ ~ ~ ~ ~ ~

*T*he days and nights are blurred together for me. *Grossmutter* patiently coaxes me to eat and nurses my unhealthy skin, but I remain listless. I sleep and stay indoors for days. I try again to heal the sheet of ice I first experienced in Vienna when I feared that *Mutti* had abandoned me. I whimper, crying for my mother. *Grossmutter* repeatedly reassures me, "Your mother and Hedi will be coming." But I do not care about my sister; I only want my mother. She is the only one who can stop the invisible bleeding in my heart.

One day, as I sit on my grandfather's knee, he talks with me, his youngest grandchild, "It's time for you to play in the sunshine. Our garden has beautiful roses blooming. We added little ceramic dwarfs. Go look at them."

I shake my head, "I want *Mutti*. When will I see her?"

"I talk with the Brapts often. Hedi is still too weak to travel. The borders are being heavily patrolled. It's too dangerous to smuggle anyone across the border now. We'll have to be patient. Now, as for you, play on the veranda and yard, but don't let anyone see you outside of the family. No matter who comes in, you must hide."

"Why? Does Theresa have to hide?"

"It's different with Theresa. They know she's my granddaughter. We don't hide her as much as we used to, when the soldiers came by often. Sometimes we still hide her. She is a young woman. When the soldiers or partisans have too much wine, it's better that she not be around. With you, it's different. I don't have permission to have you here. So, no one must know. It could be very dangerous."

"But I'm your granddaughter, too."

"I know. I know. I'll take care of it. Now you have to get stronger. Your mother sent you a message. She wants you to eat and not be so sad."

"Did she really send me that message? How? When will I see her?"

"The Brapts told me. They were here while you were sleeping. Now I want you to do as your mother says."

"She still remembers me," I feel the corners of my lips twitch into a tiny smile. The heaviness in my chest becomes a little lighter.

Slowly, I start to reacquaint myself with my cousins and surroundings. However, the internal icy walls are with me a great deal of the time, and my daily actions are mechanical.

This is an active household. It attracts the town's officials, who enjoy the hospitality and the intensely heated conversations with my grandfather. *Grossvater* is a man of strong beliefs, and an unshakable faith in God. His uncompromising convictions are laced with the ability to inspire camaraderie and deep respect. He is a great spinner of tales, making listeners laugh. He cultivates friendships with the partisans. They are welcomed whenever they appear, day or night. *Grossmutter* feeds them while *Grossvater* drinks wine and whiskey with them, swapping tales in Serbian. Often at night, German people from the camps stealthily creep to the house, begging for food. Sometimes *Grossmutter* smuggles provisions from the kitchen to the starving people of the camps, while *Grossvater* entertains the partisans in another part of the house.

Most of my time is spent hiding in the bedroom reserved for the children. I don't really understand why I have to hide. I resent it, but I sense the familiar raw fear of my cousins and grandparents. I accept their fears and do as I am told.

One Sunday afternoon, a local official, with his wife and young son, make an unexpected visit to the Westermeyer family. When the couple enters the kitchen, *Grossmutter* whisks me into the huge adjoining pantry, where I have never been. As my eyes adjust to the dimness, my heart begins to pound. Above me hang rows of smoked hams and sausages. Crocks of sauerkraut line one wall. I can hear my grandfather talking and laughing with the man and his wife on the other side of the door. On the tops of the huge, rolled-back gunny-sacks of flour and sugar rest tin scoops. Suddenly, I see a mouse jump on top of the tin scoop into the powdery white flour, while another crawls into the sugar. I gasp. My hand clamps over my mouth, muffling a scream. I back up, banging into the wall. I want to run.

"I'll get the butter from the pantry," I hear Theresa say.

"What's the matter? Stop this commotion! They'll hear you," whispers Theresa, who has entered the pantry.

"Mice. Over there. I'm afraid of mice."

"They won't hurt you. Be quiet."

"I want to go outside. I'm afraid of mice," I repeat.

"I have to go. Don't come out. The mice won't hurt you. Don't come out until I get you. It'll be soon." Theresa grabs the butter dish and dashes out.

I watch the mice. I am hot. Then I am cold. My heart pounds in my ears. I notice that there is no sound from the kitchen. I open the pantry door a crack. The kitchen is empty. I dash out, but then I hear footsteps. Too afraid of the mice to return to the pantry, I squeeze behind the kitchen door. The footsteps stop. I turn my head, and see a little black-haired boy looking at me. He is wearing neatly creased trousers and gleaming polished shoes. His dark brown eyes look eagerly at me. He speaks in a language I do not understand. I speak to him in German, then Hungarian, but he does not understand me. He twirls around, talking in what sounded like gibberish to me. In a few minutes, the boy returns, dragging his mother by the hand. The boy's father and my family follow closely behind. All stare at me. Theresa kneels next to me, "I told you to stay in the pantry. Now look what you've done."

"I was afraid of the mice."

My grandfather shakes his head with a pained expression on his face.

"Who is this child?" asks the official in a harsh voice.

"My granddaughter."

"She isn't registered. You know what the punishment is for harboring anyone without permission. You and your family are one of the few lucky families remaining in town. Your United States citizenship has protected you so far. You're my friends. I've helped you, but this I cannot conceal. It would be dangerous for my family."

"I had to help my daughter. Her children were starving. This one is such a little child. How can she be a threat to the government?"

"It's the rule. You know the law. They'll put your wife and the little children into Gakovo. You and your grandson will most likely go elsewhere," says the official. They talk for hours. Finally, it is agreed that the official will work through the bureaucratic red tape to gain permission to keep me, and to bring Hedi to Miletitsch. In the meantime, I must remain hidden. No one else must know that I am already in Miletitsch.

The days are an endless series of hiding places for me. My grandmother tries to bring some regularity to my life, but someone is always coming unexpectedly, forcing me to hide quickly. Evenings are the most frightening. I often hear men singing drunkenly. Grandfather's voice booms, arguing for a cause, his tongue loosened by alcohol.

I do not understand the language. When Grandfather gets too quarrelsome, my grandmother goes into the room to subdue him. She speaks little, but the presence of his tiny wife calms the big man.

One evening, Grandmother pushes him into the children's bedroom, which is the closest room to the kitchen. She has insisted that the others leave. Grandfather has had too much to drink, and she cannot get him beyond the bedroom. I have never seen my grandfather this drunk. Alarmed, I watch, listening to his slurred speech.

Grandmother sits him on a chair, letting him hold on to her waist. Tears stream down his leathery cheeks. "I told them not to follow Hitler. They put him before God. I told them to stay home, where they belonged, but they wouldn't listen. My friends. My childhood friends. They wouldn't listen. They hate me," he laments.

"I know. It's too late. There's nothing we can do," my grandmother soothes him.

"How could they be so stupid? How could they stop thinking? The children are all in danger. What if I can't save them? If only they had listened. No man can put himself before God." He rambles on late into the night. Theresa and Grandmother make him drink steaming cups of strong, black coffee. Eventually the two are able to guide him to his bed.

A few days later, another cousin, Leni Steiger, is added to the household. Grandfather has bribed the guards at Gakovo to release her. She has dark, curly hair and beautiful, sad, brown eyes. She is withdrawn, seldom speaking with anyone. When she wets her underpants, Grandmother kindly changes and washes her. Like me, she is small for her age, undernourished, and sickly looking. She is ten years of age, two years older than I.

Leni's family remained in Miletitsch during the war, but in July of 1945, they had been placed in camps in other towns. Her mother, Ress, was in Hodschag, her fourteen-year-old brother, Frank, was in

Doroslovo, and Leni and her grandmother had been shipped to Gakovo.

Leni and I sleep in the same bed. When I speak to Leni, she turns away in silence. Still, I am glad to have a companion when we hide. Eventually, we begin to speak to each other. I tell her about the bombings and, haltingly, Leni shares snatches of her experiences in Gakovo.

"The babies died the most. They needed food. And the old people seemed to die of sadness," Leni says one day. "Every morning, there was a death wagon. They heaped the dead bodies on the wagon. Arms, legs, and heads would hang over the sides. They buried everybody — our friends and relatives — in one grave."

I nod. "I know about babies," I say. "They get boils and die. And the mothers are sad."

~ ~ ~ ~ ~ ~

One evening, when we are eating dinner in the summer kitchen, some Serbian soldiers come for an unexpected visit. Leni and I shoot up the stairs to the attic, where the grain is stored. As usual, our grandmother feeds the visitors the family's delicious chicken goulash and potatoes. Grandfather starts drinking with them, spinning a tale of how it used to be in Miletitsch before the war.

By now, I can understand a few words of Serbian. Leni and I listen, lying on the floor so we can hear better, repeating to each other what we understand. Grandmother comes up with two slices of bread under her apron. "I'm sorry. This is all I could bring. Be quiet, just like you are. You're both such good little girls. I'll get them to go home soon. Then I'll make you a nice hot supper. They ate everything I cooked," says Grandmother. Winking to us, she goes back down the stairs.

We hear our grandmother hint to the visitors that it is getting late, that it is time to go to bed. But Grandfather has started a tale, and he insists they stay. The conversation resumes, but no one notices our grandmother taking a wicker wash basket to the attic. Upstairs, she whispers to us girls, "I'm going to take you to the front part of the house in this basket." Both of us climb in, but Grandmother can't lift the basket.

"I'll take Leni first. Then I'll come for you, Hildie. Now stop your giggling. This is serious. Those men downstairs are mean. Real mean. They act real nice to your face, but they'll knife you without blinking an eye. Real sly they are. Their eyes are always darting everywhere looking for trouble. Just you wait till I get your grandfather alone."

After Leni climbs into the basket, Grandmother covers her with a big white sheet. "Oops. Here we go. Be very quiet," says Grandmother. With heavy steps, she walks down the stairs, sneaking past the men. Most of them have their backs to her. In a few minutes, she returns. One of the men says to her, "What are you doing with that basket?"

"I'm getting the laundry from upstairs in the attic."

"Let me go with you to finish. I'll help you. You work too hard. You're just a wisp of a woman. No matter what time of day I come, you're always working. You're quite a woman," the man says admiringly.

"Thank you. No, no. I don't need your help. Just pour yourself another shot of whiskey. It's always nice to see you. How is your wife?"

"She's fine, but she's not the woman you are. She doesn't like to work too much." They both laugh, Grandmother continuing her climb up the stairs. In the attic, she wipes her brow, taking deep breaths.

"Climb in the basket, Hildie," she says. "I carried Leni. I'm sure I can carry you. Wait until I get your grandfather alone. He's going to be sorry for keeping those hooligans back when they were ready to go. Men! He forgot all about you girls. Give him a chance to tell a story, and he forgets everything. I've heard him tell that story a hundred times. Get in this basket. And, keep quiet."

Her anger seems to give her strength far beyond her normal capacity. She stumbles down the stairs, one step at a time. I see a light filter through the weavings of the basket. I hear Grandmother groan softly.

"Let me help you with that basket," says the man as before.

"No, no. I can manage," says Grandmother, but he grabs the basket from her hands. I fall to the other side of the basket. "You sure have heavy laundry," he says.

"Yes. A woman's work is never done. Just stand the basket outside the door. I'll have Theresa sprinkle it so we can iron tomorrow." Grandmother opens the door for him to set the basket outside. "You're a good man to help an old woman. Let me get some of that apple strudel you like so much. I think I have a piece left in the pantry," says Grandmother.

When I hear the door close, I crawl out of the basket, running to the children's bedroom. "Go to bed, girls. I have to see if I can help *Grossmutter*," says Theresa.

In bed, Leni says, "In Gakovo, we slept on the floor. They nailed a board across the room, put a little straw on the floor, and we all slept together. It was very crowded." Pause. "We didn't have food. My grandmother gave me hers. I miss my grandmother."

"I miss my mother," I say. Neither of us reaches out to the other. We lie lost in our separate thoughts, our bodies not touching.

Leni continues. "When someone was caught trying to escape, they locked him in the dark cellar, all naked. They made him sit naked in the cold without food and water. The basement was damp and cold." Leni pauses, then goes on, "If the guards got bored, or were mad at us, they lined everybody up in two lines, making us hit the person next to us. The old people hit the children, the children hit old people. If we didn't hit them as hard as we could, the guards hit us." Moonlight streaming across our bed, we doze, each at the opposite side of the bed.

The next day, Leni is taken to the home of another relative. She is one of the lucky ones from the camps. Grandmother tells me that with proper nutrition she will get well and strong.

~ ~ ~ ~ ~ ~

*T*he days are getting shorter now. Theresa and Grandmother close the summer kitchen, moving the pots and pans toward the front of the house into the winter kitchen.

"Hildie, I have good news for you," says Grandfather one day.

"Is *Mutti* coming?"

"No. Not yet, but soon we'll have a surprise for you. My good news is that you can go outside. You don't have to hide anymore. The Serbian officials gave us permission to keep you. It took a long time and a lot of money, but it's safe for you to be seen. Just don't wander too far from home."

Grandmother says, "The little Wardu boy down the street is the only child left around here. He's living with his grandmother. I'm sure they would welcome your company."

"May I go now?" I ask.

"After breakfast," answers Grandmother. Excited, I gulp my food down and pull on my sweater. Since I still have not learned to tie my shoelaces, Theresa ties them for me.

Outside, the town is empty and quiet, just as I remember it the last time I visited Miletitsch before the war, only one year ago. I wander through the empty homes. Most have been ransacked. What remains has been flung into all parts of the homes. I notice a curious thing. In all of the homes, no matter how messy, the holy pictures and crosses remain undisturbed on the walls. Something compels me to take a tiny, brightly colored picture of the Sacred Heart. I think of my mother as I stuff it into my sweater.

When I return home, I hide the picture under my bed, making sure no one sees me. I seem to be obsessed by the need to save these holy relics. Every day, I wander through the unoccupied homes in search of holy icons. My thoughts are always of my mother. Somehow I feel closer to my mother when I save these precious things.

During supper one evening, Grandmother asks, "Are you playing with the Wardu boy"'

"No. I haven't seen him," I answer.

"What do you do all day out there? Aren't you lonely?" asks Theresa.

"I look at the vacant homes. Are the people coming back?" I inquire.

"Maybe. We hope they come back. Of course, I don't know how many of their belongings will be left. We have a shed full of things that people asked us to save for them. *Grossvater* was angry, but how could I refuse those poor people, our friends, our relatives?" says Grandmother.

"Don't touch anything or take anything out of the homes. Remember that the things in those homes belong to the owners," cautions Grandfather. I avert my eyes from his penetrating black eyes. Sometimes I feel that he can see deep inside me. I promise myself not to take anymore holy items. But I cannot stop myself. I am drawn to them like a magnet.

Each Sunday, the handful of Roman Catholics who still remain in town go to mass. I love the huge picture of Jesus holding a lamb. I am awed by the anguished figure nailed to the cross behind the altar. Each moment is spent in prayer for my mother. I do not ask God for anything more than to take care of my mother — that she be safe and not die. Most of all, I love the painting of the Madonna and Child. When Theresa tells me that this is the mother of Jesus, a mother to all the children and people on earth, I transfer all my love to Mary. I feel guided and protected when I kneel in front of Mary's statue.

As before the war, we go to mass as a family. There are no excuses to miss mass as far as Grandfather is concerned. If one of us children says that we are too ill to attend, Grandfather will have none of it.

"You go to church. You'll feel better when you get home," his voice booms. And he is right. We always feel better after we go to mass.

Grandmother is the only one exempted from mass. She stays home, cooking and baking wonderfully delicious meals. After we have dinner, the women wash the dishes. Then everyone takes a nap, since Sundays are for resting. Grandfather is positive that God wants no work done on this day. He makes sure that no one does anything more strenuous than talking and playing games.

One Sunday after mass, Grandfather says to me, "It's high time you made your First Communion. I've talked to the priest. You and the Wardu boy will go once a week for lessons."

"Will *Mutti* be here then? I shouldn't make my First Communion without my mother," I say.

He answers vaguely, "We'll see."

My excursions into the empty homes continue. By now the pile of pictures and crosses barely fits under my bed. I lie on my stomach on the floor, shoving them back, but some slide forward. Crawling under the bed, I make neat piles of the framed pictures, but when I turn around, they slide every which way.

"What do you have under your bed?" asks Grandfather one day.

"Holy pictures and crosses of Jesus."

"Where did they come from?"

"I got them out of the vacant homes."

"Didn't I tell you not to touch anything? What will you do when the owners come back?"

"I'll give them back to them. I know which belongs to each house. Well, some do look a lot alike, but I'm sure I remember where they belong. How could they go away, leaving their holy pictures and crosses? Didn't they love God enough?"

"They were in a hurry. Seems like everybody forgot God. Why are you saving them?"

"I'm saving them for *Mutti*. She'll look at them with me. Jesus will help me to keep my mother safe."

"Yes, He will," his voice rises to a funny high pitch, cracking. He looks at me and says, "You have to eat and stop being so sad."

"I'm not hungry. I want my mother. Does she still remember me? Is she dead?"

"Of course she's not dead. She remembers you. You're her baby."

A few days after that, my grandparents bundle me into the horse-drawn carriage.

"Where are we going?" I ask, as the horses trot along the icy road. I sit between my grandparents. A thick wool blanket covers me.

"It's a surprise. We're going to visit someone special," says Grandmother. I sink back into my thoughts, praying. I spend most of my waking hours in this place—an unfeeling frozen deadness inside me. The only time I feel alive is when I collect the holy items, or when I pray to Mary's statue at church.

At the border, a sentry with a rifle slung over his shoulder speaks with my grandfather. He directs us into a hut. Despite a wood-burning stove, it is cold inside. Grimy wooden benches line the walls. I sit on a bench, only partly aware of my surroundings. Everyone seems edgy. I see Grandfather slip a roll of money to the sentry. The sentry goes outside. Returning, he shrugs his shoulders. My grandparents speak in hushed voices to each other, looking at me. I slip into my thoughts again.

Then I hear a familiar voice say, "Hildie, Hildiely." It is my mother. She tries to hug me, but I pull away. "It's me, *Mutti*. Don't you recognize me?" I shake my head, stand up, move deep into the corner of the bench.

Concerned for my sadness, my grandparents have made arrangements for me to visit my mother at the border.

"Leave her alone. She'll warm up to you. We didn't tell her we were going to meet you, because we didn't want to disappoint her in case you couldn't make it," says Grandmother, then asks, "How is Hedi?"

"Oh, Mother, it's been so hard. She's feeling better now, but she looks awful. She's growing so fast. She's going to be tall like Dad. She has his brown eyes, too. Hildie's going to be tiny like you. She has your blue eyes, you know," says my mother.

While my mother and grandmother chat, they keep glancing at me. I stare at my mother, listening to her voice. The more I recognize my mother, the more I pull out of my inner thoughts and begin to feel again. When I meet *Mutti*'s eyes, I smile. She slips me onto her lap.

"*Mutti, Mutti*," I sigh softly.

"Let's not waste our time with tears," says *Mutti*, eyeing the sentry. "Tell me what you have been doing."

"I collect holy pictures for you."

"For me? Why?"

"I want to show them to you when you come to Miletitsch. I'm going to make my First Communion. Will you be there?"

"I don't know. Pray for me and Hedi. I pray for you."

"Do you need money?" Grandfather asks my mother.

"Money is worthless. Coffee and tobacco are the best," she replies. As the adults speak, I walk around them, playing between their legs. Inside me, a prism of light shines brightly. The heaviness in my chest is gone. I feel light and happy. I laugh, hugging my mother, "I'm so glad to see you," I say affectionately.

Then the sentry walks hurriedly to the adults.

Grandfather says, "Quickly, we have to go. Another guard is coming. We can't get caught." There are hurried hugs. My mother jumps onto her wagon, heading back to Hungary. My grandparents and I race for our wagon. The horses move quickly toward home. Golden, glowing embers warm me inside. I snuggle against Grandmother's warm wool coat. The cold air feels delicious to me.

After this trip, I become interested in everything and everyone. My curiosity has returned, my appetite improves, and I play with the Wardu boy. Everything is wonderful and comparatively quiet—until throngs of strangers arrive in town.

Chapter Ten

*T*his week I am eager to begin my session with Dr. Gregg. He senses my mood and smiles.

"How was your week?" he asks.

"I have been remembering so much about our time with our grandparents in Miletitsch after the war."

"Was it a good time?"

"It was good and not so good...I was happy with my grandparents and cousins, but Miletitsch was changed after the war," I comment.

"In what way?" he asks.

"There was fear. My grandparents had to be careful to stay on the good side of the Yugoslav soldiers who patrolled the town. Our German neighbors were mostly gone, and we continued to hear about the horrors of the camps where many were held."

I pause, recollecting that interlude in Miletitsch between being a refugee and immigrating to America. I am, once again lost in my memories.

"You mentioned something about strangers arriving in the village," he prompts.

"Oh yes, the 'Kolonisten,' or colonists – peasant people who were being resettled by the government into the village. It was a strange time."

~ ~ ~ ~ ~ ~

O n foot and by wagon, the so-called *Kolonisten* arrive in Miletitsch. They are placed into the former homes of the German families who had fled, or been taken to camps. The *Kolonisten* are poor and uneducated. My grandparents warn me not to leave the house, but after a few days, I slip out. The streets are alive with olive-colored people who have black hair and dark eyes. They wear many layers of clothing, and the women wear long dresses. Many wear high-fringed moccasins that curl upward at the toes. Others are barefoot. Women walk down the street knitting. Others walk, talking in groups, twirling and spinning wool from bags slung on their backs.

The newcomers are intrigued with my blonde hair and blue eyes. Yugoslav soldiers are in charge of the resettlement. Although the soldiers behave respectfully, the remaining German families are afraid of Yugoslavs because of the rumored atrocities they have committed.

I laugh at the *Kolonistens'* ignorance of the Miletitsch way of life. A gang of children follow me wherever I go. When I discover that they have never seen a cooking stove before, and have no idea how to start a fire in it, I ask my grandfather to show them. The people are grateful. Naturally, the *Kolonisten* feel that Miletitsch is a paradise. They cannot believe their good fortune. Eventually, they ask where the former occupants of the houses are. Some carry a great deal of guilt, but others seem not to care.

Many of the former German residents had buried their valuables before they left Miletitsch. They tried to hide their treasures under-neath the hay shed or corn cribs — wherever the dirt was soft and easy to dig. They threw hay on top or stored wood piles over the hiding places. The *Kolonisten* have discovered these favorite hiding places, and pound long nails into the earth to locate the treasures. Before long, the Yugoslav soldiers collect all the bounty and organize a store where the recovered items can be purchased by the *Kolonisten*.

During the evenings, members of our family share our daily interactions with the *Kolonisten*.

"Did you see what the people next door used to store the milk?" I ask laughingly.

"No. What?" asks Nicky.

"A chamber pot."

"No!"

"Yes!" I say, pretending to vomit.

After some time, the Yugoslavs finally allow some of the German people to be brought back from the camps. Grandfather brings a groom, who lives with our family. When the workload is heavy, Grandfather hires additional workers. All the money goes to the Yugoslav officials. Slave labor is a way of life now. At the crack of dawn, Grandfather, Nicky, the old groom, and the other helpers hop on the wagon, to ride to work in the fields. At noon, they sit under a tree eating the lunch Grandmother or Theresa brings to them. At dusk, they ride home.

The *Kolonisten* have their own way of doing things. Under Communist rule, privately owned property is not possible. Everything belongs to the State. Thus their work is organized as a group effort. In the morning, those able to work straggle to the center of town, which is the square in front of the Roman Catholic church. Around nine o'clock, they amble to the fields, each carrying a hoe, spade, or sickle. By five o'clock, they are all back home. In the evenings, they dance folk dances in the square and sing songs. They seem to be a happy people.

~ ~ ~ ~ ~ ~

One day, Theresa says to me, "Tomorrow, we'll have a visitor."

"My mother?" I ask excitedly.

"No. Guess again."

"Is the visitor from Hungary?"

"Yes. And she will stay as long as you."

"Then it's my mother. I know it is."

"I didn't say it was your mother," says Theresa. But I pay no attention to this comment.

On the evening of the next day, Theresa calls me into the children's bedroom, "Look. Here is our surprise visitor."

I look at Hedi, and say, "Where is *Mutti*?"

"I'm here alone."

"Aren't you happy to see your sister? Say hello to her," says Theresa.

"I don't want her. I want my mother," I pout.

"She doesn't mean it, Hedi. She just misses your mother so much," says Theresa.

When Grandmother returns home, she cannot believe that the gaunt, tall girl is Hedi. "You've grown so tall. Oh, child, dear, dear, child. You're like a scarecrow. How is your skin?" asks Grandmother.

"All healed. Everything's better. I'm just tired and a little dizzy," says Hedi wearily. Grandmother nurses yet another child back to health.

With so many children in the household, there always seems to be one new illness after another. Theresa's fingers become infected underneath her nails. The throbbing pain makes her wince. Each day, Grandfather tells her to disinfect a needle over the fire, to prick the swollen part, then to soak her fingers in hot milk to draw out the infection. She will not let him prick her finger, and she cannot bring herself to do it. For hours, she sits with the needle poised.

"If you don't do it now, I'll do it for you," Grandfather's voice booms. She closes her eyes, sticking the pin into one finger. Then she repeats the process with the next finger and the next. She soaks her fingers in the saucer of hot milk Hedi has brought her. Over the next few weeks, she loses most of her fingernails, but the infection clears up, and healthy new nails grow.

Nicky develops a more serious ailment. Grandfather has bought a spirited young horse. He warns Nicky not to annoy the animal, but being sixteen years old, Nicky does not heed an old man. While feeding the horse, Nicky teases the animal. The horse grabs the front of his shirt, biting clear to Nicky's breastbone. The wound becomes infected.

Shortly thereafter, Nicky catches malaria. Standing in the bedroom, we children watch Grandmother wrapping cold, wet sheets around his feverish body. He kicks the sheets off, flinging himself around the bed. Grandfather helps hold Nicky down, while Grandmother puts another cold sheet around the young boy. In his delirium, he moans in English, "Mommy, Mommy, I want some ice cream." Theresa's and Nicky's mother and father are in the United States of America. The two children had come to visit their grandparents and got stranded in Miletitsch by the war. Theresa is afraid her brother will die.

"Nicky, Nicky, you have to hold on. You have to get well so that we can go home to America and see Mommy," she cries.

Grandfather turns around. "Get out of this room. All of you OUT," he roars. We three girls scurry out, and sit on the veranda underneath the window listening to Nicky's ramblings. We pray for him to get well. Over and over we repeat our prayers to God.

Toward morning, the fever breaks. Nicky lies exhausted on the bed. "Girls, come and look at Nicky. Be quiet. Don't disturb him. He's going to be fine," says Grandfather.

When Theresa sees her brother's pale body, she cries, "Oh, Nicky, Nicky. He looks awful. Are you sure he isn't going to die?"

"I think he'll be fine. I nursed many men in World War I, and I can tell. The quinine pills will help the malaria and the infection in the wound is almost all cleared up," says Grandfather. Nicky has a long convalescence under Grandmother's tender care.

~ ~ ~ ~ ~ ~

Finally, the day of my First Communion arrives. The religion classes for me and the Wardu boy are over. The priest has heard our confessions. Our souls are pure, ready to receive the Eucharist.

I question everyone, "What does the host taste like?"

Someone says, "It tastes like nothing."

Another says, "It tastes like the wafers we use for cookies."

Another says, "It tastes like cardboard."

The issue is put to rest when Theresa says, "It doesn't matter what it tastes like. It's the body and blood of Christ. It helps make you a better person and washes away your sins."

Hedi lets me wear her favorite blue taffeta dress. Although she has outgrown it, Hedi has kept it anyway. It is the prettiest dress she owns. Tiny embroidered flowers cover the bodice and collar. The puffed sleeves make me feel very pretty.

On Saturday evening, Theresa washes my hair and sets it in rags. The next morning she unwraps the rags, combing my hair into beautiful long curls that cascade down my back. On the way to church, the *Kolonisten* marvel at my beautiful dress. They are enchanted with my golden curls and love to touch them. I walk proudly to church. I toss my head back and forth to make the curls bounce, to the delight of everyone. Even Grandmother joins the family on this special day.

Inside the church, all eyes are on the young boy and me. I love the attention, turning around often from the front pew to look at the audience. Glimpsing Grandfather's stormy eyes, I quickly turn back to face the altar, listening to the priest.

"*Grossvater*'s eyes are so like *Mutti*'s," I think. "I wish *Mutti* were here." Since the priest is speaking in Latin, I do not understand him, but because I do not want to miss my cue to come forward to receive the Eucharist, I pay close attention.

When the celebration is over at the end of the day, I remember feeling pretty and being the center of attention in the beautiful church. I had waited for a stirring inside myself, but I had felt nothing special. I hope that it will come later. For now I am glad to be able join the adults each Sunday when they go to Communion.

~ ~ ~ ~ ~ ~

*O*ur grandparents are in constant fear of being placed in one of the camps. They encourage us girls to stay at home and keep off the streets. But Hedi and I like the singing and dancing of the *Kolonisten*.

One day, Grandfather comes home and says to me, "Was that you dancing the *cola* in the square?"

"Yes. I can sing many songs about Tito. My friends are teaching me the dance steps," I say, proudly.

"Didn't I tell you to stay home? No children in this house are going to dance with those people. We are different. We have different customs. We believe in God; they don't. Stay away from the square. Be careful what you say. It isn't safe here," Grandfather warns.

After that, we amuse ourselves close to home. To help our grandmother, Hedi and I are assigned the task of rolling skeins of wool into balls of yarn on the veranda. Hedi says, "I know. Let's make a web with this yarn. Pull the ball through the legs of the chair, around the columns. Take your shoes off. I'll take mine off, too. Now put the yarn through my big toe, then yours. Let's see if we can roll the yarn." By now, Hedi and I are close friends. I have fallen completely under my sister's spell. Hedi is always full of new ideas for games that make me giggle.

"Pull, pull," coaxes Hedi.

"I'm pulling, but the yarn won't budge. It tickles my toes," I laugh hilariously.

"Mine, too," says Hedi, helpless with laughter.

"What's going on here? You girls are always giggling when you should be working. Now what are you doing? What's with this yarn" scolds Grandmother.

"We...we," sputters Hedi, but we both dissolve in laughter.

"Put the skeins of yarn inside. We'll do it later. Put your shoes on. It's too cold to go barefoot," says Grandmother.

We wander into the back yard where Grandfather is shoveling the manure out of the stables, throwing new straw on the floor. Theresa is pumping buckets of water for Nicky to give to the cows.

"Want me to pump?" asks Hedi.

"Sure, if you think you can," says Theresa. Hedi strains with all her might. A trickle of water comes out of the spout.

"You're not strong enough. I'll do it."

"I can do it. I can do it. Just give me a little time," says Hedi.

"May I clean your wine bottle?" I ask Grandfather.

"If you're careful."

I run into the house, returning with a crystal decanter, which I put under the pump. Nicky says, "Oh, you'd better ask *Grossvater*. That's his favorite bottle."

"*Grossvater*, is it okay if I clean this bottle?" I ask.

"You'd better not clean that one. That's my favorite bottle."

"Please. Let me do it. Look. It's dirty on the bottom. I promise I'll be careful. It'll shine when I get done with it," I plead.

"Well, okay, but be careful," he agrees reluctantly. He rarely refuses anything we ask of him, being very fond of his three granddaughters.

"Okay, Hedi," I say. "Pump. I need water."

"You better hold on tight. That water has a lot of force," says Hedi. Our two cousins are looking on.

"Yes. Yes. I know. Pump," I say, impatiently.

Hedi pumps hard. The water gushes out, causing the decanter to slip out of my hands. Shattered crystal slivers spray over the hard cement. I am horrified.

"You broke my favorite bottle," booms Grandfather.

I am scared to death. I have never heard that tone of voice from him before. I run into the children's bedroom, slipping behind the tiled stove. I wet my underpants and suck my thumb. Everybody tries to coax me out, but I am too afraid of my grandfather grumbling outside. He has never spanked me, but I know how much the glass decanter meant to him. Hands and arms reach for me, but no one is small enough to squeeze behind the stove.

"Let her be. She'll come out by herself," says Grandmother.

But I cannot come out. I sit back there for hours. Finally, Grandmother stands in front of the yellow tiled stove, saying, "Dinner is ready. It's your favorite. *Grossvater* made fish goulash. We're all seated at the table, ready to say grace. Come on out."

I squeeze out from behind the stove. Grandmother changes my underpants and dress, and washes my face. "Now go tell your *Grossvater* you're sorry. Then sit down and eat. It's okay. He's not mad at you anymore," says Grandmother.

I walk into the completely silent kitchen. The other children's eyes follow as I circle the table to the only available seat next to Grandfather. My eyes downcast, I apologize, "I'm sorry I broke your favorite bottle. It slipped from my hand."

"It's okay. Next time you want to wash my wine bottles — don't. Anyway, I have lots more. Now sit down next to me so I can say grace," Grandfather says, winking at me.

I glance around the table once again searching for another seat away from Grandfather. My sister and cousins smirk.

"Sit down," says Grandfather with a hint of a smile.

After dinner, we girls clean the table and wash the dishes. As is our usual custom, we sing songs in harmony. Theresa has taught Hedi and me the songs she learned from her friends. She used to sing in the church choir before the war. Grandfather often sits at the table, listening. Pride shines on his face.

Just then, the gate door squeaks, and an old woman dressed in black knocks on the kitchen door. "Come in. Sit down. What news have you?" asks Grandmother.

"They're grinding glass into the food in Gakovo."

"Oh, don't talk so stupid. Did you see them do it?" asks Grandfather. Grandmother shoots him a hot glance.

"No. I didn't see it, but I know the cook. She said I shouldn't eat the food. And all the people have diarrhea. They're bleeding, and dying."

"It's probably typhoid or typhus. We had it in World War I," says Grandfather.

"Stop that, Joseph. You know we've heard that from two other people. Stop arguing," says Grandmother. To the older woman, she asks kindly, "What else is new? What's happening to the poor Oswald children?"

"Hansi got caught again smuggling people out of Gakovo. He times their escape by moonlight. With hand signals that he teaches them before leaving, he tells the groups of people what to do. The people crawl on their hands and knees. When he signals to them, they throw themselves on the ground to avoid patrols. This time, the patrols caught all of them. They know that Hansi is the leader. They'll be hard on him."

"This isn't the first time they caught him, is it? Is he safe?" asks Grandfather.

"They've caught him a few times, but he can't refuse the people when they ask him. He's a good guide. Many have escaped to Hungary because of him. He's very brave. I'm not sure he's safe. They beat him. We don't know what they do to them there. Poor boy, he's only 16."

"How is his sister, Marianne, since their mother died?" asks Grandmother.

"She is not well. She's very ill, I'm not certain that she will survive. Her brother is very caring of her, but he has not food for her and he can't replace the love of her mother."

Grandmother asks, "And you? How are you?"

"You see how I am. I'm forced to beg for food at night. If I get caught...well, let's not think of that. I need food. The children are starving. People are dying. I have to get back before daylight. Can you give me any food?" asks the old woman.

Grandmother looks at her husband.

He says, "Give her all she can carry."

To the old woman he says, "Don't come back. Tell the people to stop coming. If the soldiers see you, we'll be in the camp with you. Stop putting us in danger."

"I was careful. No one saw me. God will reward you for all the people you've helped," says the old woman.

Theresa and Grandmother wrap bundles of food into clean cloths, making knots at the top so that the old woman can carry them.

"Let me check outside first," says Grandmother. The two women leave. When Grandmother returns, she and Grandfather argue.

"I told you. No more food to the people from the camps," he says.

"I can't turn our friends away. How can you expect me to turn our friends away when they're starving. You heard. The children are dying," says Grandmother.

"Worry about your own grandchildren. Look at these four faces. You're putting them in danger. You can't give our meals to whoever knocks on the door. Our children come first. Those people are my friends and relatives, too. I'm doing everything I can to get us to America. But they can put us all into camps any time they want to. Our American citizenship will protect us only so far. Be sensible. Think, woman! Think of our responsibilities," he pleads.

"I will. I promise I will." But it is a promise she is unable to keep. Often Grandfather entertains Yugoslav soldiers in one room, and Grandmother sneaks to the back gate with bundles of food and clothing for the Germans from the camps. We grandchildren watch both sides. We fear going to the camp, but we have faith in Grandfather's ability to keep us from harm.

~ ~ ~ ~ ~ ~

Since I have to learn Serbian in school, I make it my business to teach German to the Serbian children. Each day, they sit on the gleaming, black marble stairs in front of the house, while I stand before them saying in Serbian, "Repeat after me."

In German, I sing, "Oxen, jackass, inkwell, go to school, and learn something." The Serbian children eagerly repeat the verse.

Then, Grandmother overhears the lesson from the other side of the door. "Hildie, come in here," calls Grandmother sweetly.

"Not now. I'm teaching these children German," I say.

Grandmother opens the door at the top of the marble stairs, shooing the children away. Grabbing my arm, she pulls me into the house. "What's the idea of teaching those kids that verse?" asks Grandmother.

"I'm teaching them German. You said I could," I answer.

"Who taught you that verse?"

"I made it up. Do you like it?"

"No. I don't. How can you teach them to call themselves stupid?"

"They are, aren't they? They put milk in a chamber pot. They don't know how to use a sewing machine. When they need a fabric, they rip open the down comforter, scattering the feathers all over the house, and..."

"Enough! They're not used to our ways. No more German lessons. Just hope they don't repeat it to any of their people who can understand German."

"I like being the teacher."

"Teach them — but nothing unkind. Teach them arithmetic."

"That's a good idea. I'll get the children," I say, dashing to look for my friends.

~ ~ ~ ~ ~ ~

O n the first of May, the town holds a parade. Hedi and one of her classmates are assigned the honor of carrying a huge picture of Tito. When the picture becomes too cumbersome, Hedi says to her friend, "I'll be glad when this day is over. This picture is heavy."

The next day, an official complains to Grandfather that Hedi has been disrespectful to Tito. Her girlfriend told her father of Hedi's remark, who reported it to the official. Our grandfather assures him that Hedi meant no disrespect. After all, Tito is a great man. The official is still irate. Fearing for our safety, Grandfather takes us to a farm far away from Miletitsch for a few weeks. When we return, we rarely play with the *Kolonisten* children.

As in the past, each day in the morning and evening, the town crier walks through town ringing his bell, announcing the news. One day, he announces that all young men and women between the ages of 14 and 17 should meet in the town square the next day with enough warm clothing for ten days. It is a bitter cold winter. Fear grips our household.

Grandfather speaks with the officials, but no exceptions are to be made. However, they assure him that this is just a work detail; the young people will return. All day and late into the night, *Grossmutter* washes woolen sweaters, mittens, socks, and caps and dries them by the stove.

Theresa and Nicky select the warmest, lightest garments. Nicky, at 16, has been away from home to attend school in Apatine, a private school where boys prepare for higher education. But Theresa, at 18, has led a somewhat sheltered life. She also left home to be educated by the nuns in a convent. This was not uncommon, for women in small towns were trained mostly in the genteel arts of sewing, cooking, and embroidery. Understandably, both cousins are anxious about the order to leave the village. Our grandparents worry about Theresa because she is not robust. On those rare occasions when she helps in the fields during harvest time, she invariably must return home feeling ill and is confined to bed for a few days of rest.

While Nicky and Theresa are gone, our grandparents fret day and night. Grandmother reminds Hedi and me to pray for them before going to bed. At grace before meals, Theresa and Nicky are included in the prayers, and each family member beseeches God to keep them safe. When Grandmother speaks, she sometimes breaks down in tears. She works as if possessed to keep herself occupied. Grandfather is grouchy, snapping at his wife. He is more determined than ever to relocate his family in America.

Grandmother says, "In America, the streets aren't paved in gold and money doesn't fall off the trees, but your shoes never get dirty like in Miletitsch. You go to the store to buy anything you need. You can talk and go to church without being afraid. In Chicago, where we lived, people minded their own business and left you alone."

Ten days later, Nicky and Theresa return to Miletitsch. Although covered with mud from head to toe, underfed, and infested with head lice, they seem none the worse for their experience. After the initial emotional greetings, they are stripped of their clothing and bathed. *Grossmutter* washes their heads and douses them with kerosene. Our entire family returns to the ritual of using a fine-toothed comb again as a preventive measure to avoid becoming infected with head lice.

On their first evening back home, we feast on a dinner of liver dumpling soup, fried chicken, parsley potatoes, homemade bread, and apricot jelly roll, washed down with glasses of fresh milk.

My two cousins tell their stories. When they left the square in front of the church, they had to walk for hours to Doroslovo in the cold, biting wind. They worked in the factory to make bricks. At night, they sang songs, crying from homesickness. The *Kolonisten* and Germans were treated equally, but Nicky and Theresa bristled at being treated as servants. They slept on the floor with a little bit of straw. Cold penetrated deep inside their bones. Aside from the fear of the unknown, which was great, the two felt humiliated, wanting to return home as quickly as possible to America. Seven years in Miletitsch had been enough for them.

~ ~ ~ ~ ~ ~

*W*inter passes. Spring rains bring tender shoots of lush, green grass. The Easter season strengthens our family's belief in rebirth and the hope for redemption. Because the priest has gone, mass, confession, and communion are no longer a part of the fabric of our lives. But the hundreds of years of beliefs, traditions, and rituals are so deeply ingrained that our family clings to them without interruption. Our household is an oasis where the belief in God permeates our daily actions and thoughts. Being surrounded by suspicious non-believers makes our fear of the camps ever greater.

We observe Lent. On Good Friday and Holy Saturday, we fast. Only boiled corn kernels are allowed on these days. The drama of the Way of the Cross is repeated. It is emphasized how gladly Jesus accepted the agony of the crown of thorns and the torture of dragging the heavy cross through Jerusalem, and, finally, being nailed to the cross. *Grossmutter* tells us how Jesus sacrificed his life to save the poor sinners on Earth. I find the agony and pain of Jesus almost unbearable, but the Resurrection lifts my spirits greatly.

For Hedi's and my sake, Theresa is determined to continue as many of the traditions as possible. She encourages us to build Easter nests.

"Why should we make nests? There is no Easter Bunny," says Hedi."

"How do you know?" retorts Theresa.

"And there is no *Christkindle*."

Theresa glances at me. I am closely following the exchange between the two.

"You've got such a fresh mouth. There is too an Easter Bunny," says Theresa. To me she says, "Just make a nice nest. You'll see, the Easter Bunny will come. I promise. I know what I'm talking about."

"Don't be ridiculous. Making a nest is a waste of time," says Hedi.

"The Easter Bunny will come. He only leaves candy for those who make nests," Theresa says pointedly to Hedi.

"I don't know how to make a nest," I say excitedly at the mention of candy.

"Just take a few bricks under that big walnut tree by the fence and build a little house. I have to go to the kitchen. Don't disturb me," Theresa says sternly. To Hedi she says, "That especially means you. I'm the oldest. You have to listen to me this time. Don't ruin it. Little children should enjoy Easter."

Running over the wet, soft grass, I carry a brick to the walnut tree.

"I'm not making a nest. Don't be silly," Hedi says to me.

To me, Theresa says, "Only those children who make nests will receive candy from the Easter Bunny. It's your decision." Theresa leaves, locking herself in the kitchen to ensure that her promise of candy would be fulfilled.

"I'm making a nest," I say, carrying another brick. I am unsure if there is an Easter Bunny. Hedi seems so positive; she is wise about such things. But Theresa says there will be candy only for the children with the nests. I trust Theresa in matters relating to candy. A few more bricks. I am so absorbed in the intricacies of building a nest that I no longer hear my sister's rational explanations of reality.

Nicky and Grandmother join Hedi and me. "I can't make a nest. I don't know how," I say, sitting on the wet grass, frustrated with the pile of bricks in front of me.

"You're getting all wet and muddy," says Grandmother.

Irritated by Grandmother's constant concern for cleanliness, I fling myself up, then drop to my knees.

"Don't bother with a nest, then. Maybe the Easter Bunny will leave candy under your bed," says Grandmother.

"See, I told you it was silly to build a nest," says Hedi. "You'll get your candy anyway. I'll get it and I'm not building a nest."

"Leave me alone. I want a nest. I want to build a house." My impatience turns to anger. The tall stack of bricks tumbles over.

Nicky kneels next to me. "Here. Let me help you. All you need is four bricks."

"Let me do it. Don't do it for me. I want to do it by myself," I say, frustrated.

So Nicky instructs me, "Place two bricks next to each other, but leave a little room between. Then place two bricks on top. There, now you have a house. You can return those other bricks where you got them."

"That's a nest? This is much too small. The Easter Bunny can't put much candy in this tiny hole," I say. Theresa joins the group.

I ask anxiously, "Is this big enough for the Easter Bunny?"

"It's fine. If it doesn't fit, he can always lay the candy on top," smiles Theresa. Hedi sneers. I take one more brick, "This will be the door. Think he can open it?"

"I'm sure he can. Come, Hedi and Nicky, let's put these bricks back for Hildie," says Theresa, satisfied that her little cousin had reentered a special place reserved for childhood.

I play for hours readjusting the five bricks. I line the inside and top of the bricks with fresh, sweet-smelling grass. Early the next morning, I jump out of bed. Barefoot, in my nightgown, I run to the nest. It is filled with poppy seed candy and caramelized sugar with walnuts wrapped in brightly colored paper. Hard-boiled, tan Easter eggs that look like sandy beaches, which had been soaked in onion skins, are nestled in the back, along with a bright yellow apple. I share the candy with my cousins and my sister, hoarding the rest under my bed.

Later, Grandfather reads out loud from the big holy book. The family's dates of births and deaths are recorded on the first few pages. Often we children pore over the pages, running our fingers over the names of our parents and our own birth dates. Visitors drop by to partake of Grandmother's cookies and cakes. She and Theresa have baked for a week. Grandfather serves his best wine, which he has saved for this special holiday.

~ ~ ~ ~ ~ ~

Since I no longer play with the *Kolonisten* children, I spend most of my time exploring or playing with Frank Wardu, who is two years younger than I. Our favorite place to play is the chapel and the adjoining cemetery. The newcomers in town avoid this area, leaving us the freedom to run and speak our thoughts in German. We play hide-and-go-seek games among the gravestones.

When the *Kolonisten* bury their dead, it is their custom to place food on the grave. Spying a funeral procession, Frank and I run to the cemetery, hanging behind the mourners.

"Remember to smile and be polite," I whisper to Frank.

After the last mourners leave, we circle the newly dug grave. We taste the food left there on a plate.

"Oh, it's sweet. I think it's honey and rice," says Frank. We suck the honey, spitting out the rice. We make a game to see who can spit the farthest.

"Look under the plate—there's money," I exclaim. "They left money for the dead!" We roll on the grass, laughing uncontrollably.

"You take the money," says Frank.

"No. I don't want it. But if we leave it, it'll get all wet. It won't be much good to anyone, especially the dead," I say. We hold each other giggling.

"It's getting dark. I have to go home," I say. "I'll take this one dinar, and you take one. And, better not tell your grandmother," I add. I stuff the money into the pocket of my sweater.

"Bye," we say to each other, racing to see who could run faster.

The next day Grandmother says to me, "Come with me." She takes my hand, escorting me to the winter kitchen. Sitting next to Grandfather, who is at the head of the table, are three *Kolonisten*. The woman wearing an ankle-length dress looks familiar to me.

"Where were you yesterday afternoon?" asks Grandfather sternly in German.

"I was playing with Frank Wardu," I answer.

"Where were you playing?"

"In the cemetery."

"What were you doing there?" he roars, from deep within his chest.

"We played hide-and-go-seek."

Stormy clouds form in his dark eyes. "Among the gravestones? What else did you do?"

"Nothing."

"Did you take the food off the grave?"

"Yes."

"What did you do with it?"

"We ate it. It was sweet. We spit out the rice. Don't they know that dead people don't eat?"

Grandfather's big hands twitch, but his voice is calm now. "Tell me that you did not take the money."

"Well, yes." A peal of laughter bubbles up inside me at the absurd custom, but my grandfather's presence suppresses it into a crooked grin.

"You stole the money?" he asks, as a hurt look shot across his face.

"I didn't steal. It didn't belong to anyone. Dead people don't need money," I try to explain, alarmed that he would think that I had broken one of the Ten Commandments. I can see how much this is hurting my beloved grandfather. He has to understand. I explain again, "I didn't steal. It was left outside for anybody to take. If it rained, the food would have washed away, and the money would be ruined."

"Where is the money?" asks Grandfather, anguish in his voice.

I dig it out of my sweater pocket, placing it in the palm of his tough, calloused hand. He says to Grandmother, "Make bundles of food for these poor people."

In Serbian, he apologizes to the people, "Please forgive my granddaughter. She meant no harm. She didn't understand your custom. She meant no disrespect to the dead."

But the Serbian woman says, "You wanted the money. That's how come you're so rich. You steal from us poor folks."

"I knew nothing of what she and the boy were doing. Nothing. Believe me," Grandfather answers. I know he has always taken great pride in his reputation for honesty.

I come to his defense. "He didn't know. I never told him. My grandfather would never let me steal. You must believe me," I say in Serbian, moving toward the three.

"Keep away from us. You have no respect for the dead," the Serbian woman says contemptuously, starting to sob. Grandfather clears his throat noisily, "How much money did you leave?"

"Ten dinar," says one of the men.

"Here is twice that amount." Grandfather takes the money out of his trouser pocket, pressing it into the man's hand. "Take this food my wife brought in. If there is anything we can do, tell me. Forgive my granddaughter; sometimes she's not too smart. I know she didn't mean to add to your grief. Hildie, apologize to these good people."

"I'm sorry. I won't eat the food or take the money anymore," I say. At that moment, the grief on the woman's face pierces my heart.

Grandfather looks at me and says, "And you will never – do you hear me? – NEVER play in that cemetery again." His loud voice bounces off the walls and ceiling. Even the grieving woman stops her moaning and sobbing.

I shrink backward. "I won't go back," I say feebly.

Grandfather escorts the *Kolonisten* to the front door. On the way back, I watch him walk by the kitchen. His shoulders are stooped. His crippled leg drags as he walks toward the vineyard in the back of the house. He does not have dinner with the family that evening, even though Grandmother urges him to join, in a hushed tone. He works in silence late into the night. He avoids me, never mentioning the cemetery incident again.

I feel crushed. I know I have disappointed him. I love him so much. He has always been kind to me. I follow him around, watching him while he does his chores. Neither of us speaks. When he tends the horses, I enter the barn. This is a place I have never been before. The strange smells and textures of the hay, straw, and rough-hewn beams distract me. The sound of the oats hitting the pail focuses my attention on my grandfather's big work-worn hands. The horse backs up.

I am afraid. I leave. Everyone in the family is aware of the distance between the two of us. We all eat dinner the next evening in strained silence. I steal glances at him, but he keeps his eyes on his plate. In the past, I could tease him into laughing, but I know that this is too serious for teasing.

After the dishes are washed, I stand in the summer kitchen doorway watching my grandfather. The bright, electric light pours into the dark back yard, framing my body. He ties the front paws of a dead rabbit together, hanging it on a peg.

"You'd better go," he says coldly. I shake my head. He glides the knife around the rabbit's fur. "You better go. You don't want to see this," he says, his hands at the rabbit's neck. Unmoving, I watch him. With a jerk he pulls the skin down, exposing the bloody carcass.

"Oh, no. What happened?" I clutch my stomach.

He walks over, putting his arms around my shoulders. "I told you not to look." I put my arms around his waist, burying my face in his stomach. A warm feeling envelops us; the coldness is gone.

Chapter Eleven

I *know that my work with Dr. Gregg is coming to a close. The flashbacks have subsided. The painful process of telling my story has been healing. I sit opposite him feeling the sun streaming in through the window.*

"What about your reunion with your mother?" asks Dr. Gregg.

After these months of reliving the experiences of separation and fear and chaos, I am somehow taken aback by his question about reconnecting with my mother after the war. My mind is blank as I try to recall.

"How was it for you when you reconnected with your mother? Perhaps you don't remember. . . ." he suggests.

But I do remember the feeling of relief and gratitude when arrangements were in place for our move to the United States. And I remember the excitement and anxiety of the journey. . . .

~ ~ ~ ~ ~ ~

*I*n August 1946, we receive word in Miletitsch from my mother, who is still in Hungary, that arrangements have been made for us to go to the United States of America. My grandparents are greatly relieved because they have been in a constant state of distress, worrying what would happen to Hedi and me if they and our cousins, Nicky and Theresa, received their immigration papers first. Now, however, there is concern about our getting to Bacsalmas, Hungary, to meet my mother in time to board the ship for America.

Grandfather again meets with the Brapts and pays them an exorbitant sum to smuggle Hedi and me across the border from Yugoslavia to Bacsalmas. Mr. Brapt is reluctant to undertake such a dangerous mission. Although Grandfather understands the danger, he has no choice, because it is our only hope of avoiding the camps.

The night before Hedi and I are to leave, Grandmother carefully lays out what each of us should wear and starts to pack. "Remember, Mr. Brapt said to pack only a small suitcase. No more," says Grandfather. Theresa and Grandmother look to each other for support.

"That's not very many clothes. What will they wear on the trip?" says Theresa.

"Well," reasons Grandmother, "we'll just pack one little bag; the rest the girls will wear in layers. They need clothes." She went on, "What do men know? It's just as dangerous with one layer of clothing, as it is with five or ten."

Hedi and I go to bed, but are unable to sleep for a long time. We hear doors open and close. We listen to our grandparents talking back and forth for hours, but the walls muffle their voices, making it impossible for us to understand. It seems that no sooner have we fallen asleep than we are awakened. Outside it is dark and silent. Breakfast is a strained, quiet affair.

In the bedroom, Theresa says to Grandmother, "First, let's put these dresses on that I made for them." She runs her fingertips over the red embroidered initials that had been such a challenge for her to sew. The white pique material was hard to work with. She is so proud of the finished product. She made the patterns for both dresses, cut out the snowy white material, sewn them, and trimmed the edges and pockets with red stitches. Theresa helps us slip our dresses over our heads, buckling our red belts.

"They do look beautiful. You did such a nice job," says Grandmother. The praise pleases Theresa.

Layer upon layer, Hedi and I pull on dresses, blouses, and sweaters, topping the ensemble with winter caps, coats, and leggings.

"Are you ready?" Grandfather calls. "They have to leave while it's dark." As we walk out of the bedroom, he asks, "What's wrong with the girls?"

"Why do you ask?" inquires Grandmother.

"Their arms are sticking out. They're so fat. You can't send these girls away like that. They can't move," says Grandfather, patting our bulky arms and sides. Hedi and I giggle. We feel like big, bulky snowmen.

A knock on the door by Mr. Brapt reminds us of the seriousness of this situation. He says, "Hurry. I can't wait one more minute. I can't do it. I just can't do it. We're going to get caught."

"Don't panic. We have a good plan. Just don't get excited. Stay calm," says Grandfather. To us, he says, "Let's go. Hurry!" We can barely move, so Theresa grabs Hedi's arm on the one side, and Grandmother grabs the other. Together, they pull Hedi out of the door. Grandfather heaves me under his arm and deposits me next to Hedi on the back of the wagon. We lay like two lumps of blubber, unable to move or sit. Before Mr. Brapt conceals us with a cover to protect us from the probing eyes of the townspeople, we whisper hurried goodbyes.

"Say hello to your *Mutti*. We'll see you in America! *Auf Wiedersehen*."

A short distance outside of town, Mr. Brapt pulls down the cover. Gratefully, we suck in the cool fresh air. The wagon resumes its race with the coming dawn. We bounce back and forth, up and down, in the back of the wagon, completely at the mercy of the road since we are unable to hold on to cushion our movements. At last, the wagon stops.

"Not one word from you girls. Don't move. Keep yourselves covered. I'll be back. Don't move," says Mr. Brapt, nervously grabbing a large jug as he walks away. Time passes.

"What are you doing?" I ask Hedi.

"I'm taking this cover off. It's too hot," says Hedi.

"Mr. Brapt said not to."

"I don't care. It's too hot," says Hedi, rolling herself from side to side under the cover.

"He said not to move." I say again.

With her hands supporting her bulky form, Hedi scoots herself to the side of the wagon, and pulls herself into a semi-sitting position, her legs sprawled out in front of her. With her feet, she kicks the cover off me. "I'm going to hold on like this, while he's driving. It's ridiculous to bounce all over like two balls," says Hedi, draping one arm over the sideboard.

I lay flat on the floor of the wagon, spreading my arms and legs away from my body, looking like an X. "Where did he go?" I ask.

"Up there. In that hut on the hill. See the light?"

I wriggle to the sideboard and peep out between the cracks. "It's almost daylight. Why doesn't he come back?"

"Could be trouble. Let's not talk anymore. Someone may hear us," cautions Hedi.

Lying on my back, I look into the light of the waxing sun. I rub my head back and forth along the rough wooden floor until my cap turns sideways, exposing my ear. Content that I could hear, I listen to the birds chirping, and the swooshing of the wind in the trees. Drunken singing and loud voices waft from the thatched hut. I scoot myself along the floor until I sit next to Hedi behind the driver's seat. It seems like a long time before two men stagger out of the hut, exchanging loud farewells. Mr. Brapt waves to the sentry, who steadies himself on the doorframe, his gun slung across his back. Mr. Brapt runs to the wagon and grabs the reins.

Then suddenly we hear, "*Stoy! Stoy!*" The soldier is shouting for Mr. Brapt to stop, pointing to the back of the wagon. He fumbles with his gun, but he loses his balance and falls to his knees.

"Hold on," calls Mr. Brapt to us, as he whips the horses. The wagon shoots forward at breakneck speed, bouncing us from one end to the other.

~ ~ ~ ~ ~ ~

$\mathcal{W}$hen we arrive in Hungary, *Mutti* has already packed and is ready to leave, but Hedi and I have perspired so much that our clothing has to be washed, and we have to be bathed again.

The trip from Hungary to Paris is another series of rides on overcrowded trains, missing connections, and dragging luggage from one point to another. Although the fear of bombings is gone, there is the panic that we will be too late and the ship will sail without us.

Paris is festive. People mingle and laugh in the square in front of Notre Dame, where they greet one another with high emotion. I can always recognize when French people meet because they kiss first one cheek then the other. I have never seen men kiss before, and find this custom most interesting. On our first day in Paris, we go to the American consulate. Inside, the rooms are full of people nervously milling about and standing in long lines waiting to speak with an official.

Suddenly we hear a man's voice call, "Kathe! What are you doing here?"

"Joseph!" shouts *Mutti*. They embrace, laughing and talking non-stop. "These are my daughters. Girls, this is your *Onkel* Wester-meyer, my brother."

We look at him intently. We figure he must be important, since our mother is so excited to see him.

"How is it that you're in Paris? Shouldn't you be in school in Nurnberg?" asks *Mutti*.

"There is nothing for me in Germany," he says. "And our home in Hungary — or I guess it's Yugoslavia now — is no place for any of us anymore. So I figured, I'll go back to Chicago. Mary and Joe are still there. I got word that Mom, Dad, Theresa, and Nicky hope to be there soon. I should get a good job since I'm an electrical engineer now. Back to Chicago — gangsters and all!" he laughs. "Have you regis-tered yet? The next ship to leave is the troop transport, the *U.S.S. Ernie Pyle.*"

"I haven't done a thing. We just got here," says *Mutti*.

"You're in the wrong line. First you have to go to the third floor. Come on. I'll show you. May I hold your hand, Hildie?" asks Uncle Westermeyer politely.

When I shyly slip my hand into his, I like how it feels. Something tells me that I am going to like this Uncle Westermeyer.

The four of us are inseparable while we are in Paris. We go to the consulate and eat our meals together. Then we visit Notre Dame. The silence inside the church is a welcome relief to me. The enormous hall is encircled by high Gothic windows, most of which have been damaged during the war and boarded up. Only one small rose-patterned glass window remains intact. I survey the massive, dim, high-ceilinged hall and feel very small. I feel comforted to be in a church again.

My mother and uncle point out details. Uncle explains the pointed arch, flying buttress, and rib vault construction. Remembering my Easter nest, I try my best to comprehend his constant flow of information about this building. I do not understand much, but I am enthralled by his energy and expansive knowledge. I think he is the smartest man in the world.

~ ~ ~ ~ ~ ~

*W*hen the *Ernie Pyle* sails from the Port of Le Havre, it carries the hopes and dreams for a better life for the war-ravaged people onboard. During the voyage, I spend my time with either my mother or uncle, or sitting on the deck. I watch the endless, rhythmic waves of the Atlantic Ocean that touch the sky in all directions. Everything is strange to me on board the ship, except for the sleeping quarters. Men and women are placed in two-tiered beds in separate rooms. The air is foul because so many are unwell when they boarded, and others have become seasick.

Outside, in the salty brisk air, I forget about the quarters below. I am fascinated with a school of graceful, gray creatures leaping in arcs across the water. People say that the dolphins are a good omen; they bring good luck. Evenings are often heralded with glorious sunsets flooding the skies in a symphony of color — scarlet-orange, misty pink, or purple-red. On special evenings, the moon casts a shimmering light on the undulating ocean. I especially like it when a fine spray splashes my face, sending a shiver of delight down my spine.

But the finger of death shadows the refugees. I stand on deck, watching a long dark rectangular bag being hoisted up by two sailors. One sailor seems ill at ease and keeps looking at my solemn face. He shouts at me, but I do not understand English.

A woman next to me says in German, "They want you to leave."

"Why?"

"They don't want you to see this burial."

"Why not?" I ask, planting my feet more firmly on the deck. The shroud bundle slides over the deck railing into the sea. After the sailors stand a moment in silence, one speaks with the woman next to me.

The woman then says to me, "He asks that you not watch the burials at sea. I guess he thinks it's not good for you. How many have you seen?"

"Three, maybe four," I say. "Soon another black flag will fly off the pole up there. Why are they dying? There are no bombings, and there is food here."

"We are all undernourished and ill. The food on the ship is too rich for us. Some are just too weak to make this journey to freedom," answers the woman.

I nod. I understand death. The sadness of the war comes back. The wounds are always festering and painful within me.

The roll of the ship makes *Mutti* ill, so she rarely comes up on deck. But on the last day, there is such an air of excitement that she cannot stay below. She steadies herself on the railing of the top deck, while I hover, ready to hold her should she become faint. The dark circles under her eyes and her yellowish complexion worry me. I have never seen her so sick or weak.

At last we arrive in New York harbor.

"Look, Hildie," says *Mutti*, smiling weakly. "That's the Statue of Liberty. We made it. We're safe. Now you will become an American girl. You will learn to speak English, and we will only speak English at home, no more German. You'll go to school. We will have a better life."

I do not like the thought of having to learn yet another language, but I do like the idea of a better life.

~ ~ ~ ~ ~ ~

I walk out of Dr. Gregg's office as usual. I have told him about my new job and planned move back to Chicago.

On the threshold, I turn around. He is in the shadows looking at me.

"Oh," I half whisper, suddenly realizing the significance of this moment. "This is the last time I'll see you, isn't it?"

He nods. We pause and then hug warmly.

"You take good care of yourself," I manage to say in a strangled voice. "You help so many people; just remember to take care of yourself." I don't know what he says or does. Blinded by tears, I turn and walk to the car.

Inside my car, I sob, and then I drive away. I know this is an ending to an important part of my life. And it is another new beginning.

Epilogue in Three Voices

Epilogue 1: Hedi

*W*hen Hildie wrote the first draft of the manuscript, she wanted to include a brief description of each of our adult lives. We tinkered with that over the years but never completed it. Here is my best attempt.

Mother, Hildie, and I arrived in New York in September 1946, about a year before our grandparents Westermeyer and our cousins, Theresa and Nick. Coming to the USA was a tremendous joy to us.

We basically set ourselves to assimilation right away. Speaking only German, Hungarian, and Serbian, we had to learn English. In those early years, Mother insisted that we speak only English at home. The principal of Knickerbocker Elementary School in Chicago, Illinois, met with Hildie and me daily to teach us this new language. The 'th' sound was one of the challenges we often laughed about. It always felt like sticking out the tongue was required to say it correctly.

Housing in Chicago was scarce after World War II and a friend of the family and her son took us in for a few months. We felt pure delight when we were eventually able to have our own apartment. It was a feeling we never forgot. We shared our home with Uncle Joseph Westermeyer for a while. At some point both our cousins, Theresa and Nick, joined us, too.

Years later, when we had a two-flat house, my grandparents lived in the downstairs of our house. After the experience of being homeless during the war, having "our" place again filled us with tremendous gratitude. In all these years since then, we have never taken home for granted. It has always been of great importance to us.

My mother worked hard. At first, she did piece work in a Mixmaster factory. Later she worked in a printing company as an offset stripper. We all got a kick out of saying that she was a "stripper" when asked about her work—followed by uproarious laughter when we saw people's facial expressions.

She had her human frailties and shortcomings, but she was definitely a woman before her time. She was courageous, competent, and strong-willed. She was also a great money manager and a risk taker. Of our immigrant group, she was the first to buy a house. And, it was no small feat, years later at around age 50, for her to buy a car and learn to drive. In 1968, at the age of 55, she died of breast cancer. During her last months, she lived with Hildie and her family in Chicago. Both of us were with her the last couple weeks of her life and when she made her final transition.

While going to school, Hildie and I both had part-time jobs. Early on it was babysitting, then working in a bakery and other things. What we earned went to our mother. As a group, we decided about purchases, often layaways, and the general management of the money for all three of us. Some things, like a new Easter hat and maybe coat, were a given.

Even though there were struggles, the prevailing feeling of gratitude for our good fortune and for being in the USA never left us. We were glad of the opportunity to work hard to create a good life. Great emphasis was always placed on education. The privilege of pursuing this was strong in both Hildie and me.

Hildie married Joseph Klemm at age 20. They had three children: Kenneth and Susan who survive, and a third child, Christopher, lived only a few hours after birth. This great loss stayed with Hildie throughout her life. I continue to be in close, loving relationship with Susan and Kenneth, who have always been dear to my heart.

While being a stay-at-home mom, in the later 1970s, Hildie earned her Bachelor's degree from Mundelein College in Chicago. Later, in 1986, her husband's work took them to Louisiana, where she pursued her Master's degree. As part of that undertaking, she wrote the first draft of this book.

In 1988, Hildie and Joe divorced. She returned to Chicago and worked as the Executive Director of the American Association of Orthopedic Surgeons until her retirement, at which time she moved to Charlotte, North Carolina, to be near her daughter, Susan.

Hildie was a woman of faith, first as a Roman Catholic and eventually as a member of the Religious Society of Friends, the Quakers. She was active at the unprogrammed Evanston, Illinois Meeting and then at the Charlotte, North Carolina Meeting. Her membership in the Meeting and her relationships with Friends supported her deepening faith.

In 2005, Hildie was diagnosed with pancreatic cancer. She did well for about 18 months and we hoped it was a miracle. Sadly, after six months of a difficult time, two years after her diagnosis, she died on May 29, 2009, at the age of 71.

My path led me to pursue nursing. I graduated as a registered nurse from the Grant Hospital School of Nursing, Chicago, Illinois, in 1956. The school no longer exists. Then I earned my bachelor's degree from DePaul University in Chicago. Later, in 1974, I received my master's degree in Mental Health/Psychiatric Nursing from the University of Wisconsin, Madison. Eventually I became a board certified, advanced practitioner.

I was married for 12 years and moved to Wisconsin. We had no children. After my divorce in 1972, I pursued graduate school and eventually established a private counseling practice. As a result of uterine cancer in 1976, I entered a journey of healing through mind, body, and spirit approaches, which set me on a lifetime course in that direction. Over the years, I have studied many spiritual teachings and paths to healing. I continue to study the Ancient Wisdom Teachings. I am also an active member of the Religious Society of Friends, Quakers. At present (2012), I live in Charlotte, North Carolina. I teach psychosynthesis and meditation, conduct retreats, and see a few clients privately for counseling and spiritual direction.

I feel blessed with all that life has brought me. This is not to minimize all that happened during the war, nor a number of other difficult life challenges. It's that I see life full of purpose and meaning. Each experience provides an opportunity for learning and evolving. Life is a great mystery — an adventure in which I feel fully engaged.

Hildie and I were close sisters all of our lives. Even though we had to deal with some bumps along the way, we always felt that we were blessed with our relationship as sisters. When living apart, we sometimes phoned daily. We could never imagine life without each other, but we would hasten to reassure each other that we would be fine if one of us died. We always assumed that I would die first.

We lived together here in Charlotte since 2005, after I moved from Madison, Wisconsin. I think we never quite adjusted to the fact that she was dying first. In looking at this whole cycle, I'm eternally grateful for our living together, making it possible for her to be at home in the environment she loved till the very end. Life takes these unexpected turns and I marvel at the way it all works, hopefully for the benefit of a greater good.

Hildie became a strong woman with a clear sense of herself to whom family was primary. She was the one who kept us all connected. Even though we are fine, we all miss her and think of her being in a peaceful, gentle place as she always wished for our little planet.

Hedwig Weiler, Hildie's Sister

Epilogue 2: Susan

First, I want to express thanks to those who read this book. My hope is that it helps document history and in so doing, may perhaps change the future. This book serves also as a thank you to the many people who have helped my family over the years—kind strangers, teachers, doctors, clergy, friends, and family. We appreciate the kindnesses and generosities that have contributed to the healing of my mother and our entire family. Often it is the small kindnesses that make huge differences—a bowl of soup, a kind word, a smile. Upon arriving in the United States, my family was helped by many people, and we are grateful for their generosity to us during a difficult time.

Friends who have read early versions of this book have expressed interest in what happened in my mother's life after she arrived in the United States. Here is that part of my mother's story as I know it.

She and her sister and mother settled in Chicago. Life was difficult as the struggle for survival in a new land took place amidst the raw spots and trauma of the refugee years. For my mother, this was bound with being a child of divorce and living in a single-parent household. My grandmother worked very hard to make life as nice as she could for the family. "Nice" in our culture means many things— buying the best you can; finding flowers for the table; celebrating holidays with family; putting out a white table cloth and good china; cooking and baking; giving gifts of jewelry to mark birthdays and graduations. Each piece of a new life was constructed. In our family there was a deep gratefulness to be American, to live in a land that was peaceful, and to have the opportunity to work and create a good life.

My grandmother's dreams for my mom were for her to be a model and a secretary. My mother accomplished both of these things early on. She was an executive secretary by the time she reached her early twenties. She met my father when they were both eighteen. His family had recently immigrated to Chicago also. In fact, my mother's grandfather sponsored them. My mother and father met while my mother was hanging curtains in an apartment being set up for my father's family.

They married when they were 20 years old, and soon thereafter, my father enlisted in the United States Army. During his time in the Army, he was stationed in Germany, and so my mother lived there with him for 18 months. My brother, Kenneth, was born when my parents were 25, and I came along when they were 27. My mother stayed at home with us.

My father also was a child of war, and while his situation had been more stable than my mother's, it was traumatic for him also. My parents (and the world as a whole) had limited understanding of the long-term impact of early trauma. While the outer circumstances of their lives had improved, the effects of their wartime experiences as children were still virulent in their lives. So these two fine people came together in a marriage in a new culture. But in many ways, they were ill equipped to build relationship — despite their basic decency, their genuine belief in God, and their continual striving.

My parents were Catholic, and our family went to religious classes and church weekly. Both my parents instilled in my brother and me a deep belief in a compassionate God upon whom one could call at anytime. During the 1980s, my mother began meeting with the Society of Friends, Quakers. The quiet Quaker meetings deepened her understanding of the God of all creation and became a crucial part of her life.

My mother was diagnosed with breast cancer at the age of 55. During her successful recovery, she began a creative healing process of artistic expression. This creative process grew stronger and stronger and became a mainstay of her life from that time on. To her, each painting or sketch held healing power for the person for whom it was created — as well as for those who basked in the presence of a piece of her art. Her paintings are on display in the Hickory Grove

Public Library in Charlotte, North Carolina and in the Evanston Meeting House in Evanston, Illinois.

In her retirement, my mother lived here in Charlotte, North Carolina. During these later years, her commitment to this book and to her healing art grew, as did her commitment to being present and supportive to my brother and me. She came to love Charlotte during the time she lived here. Over the years, her relationship with her cousins, who were still in Germany, continued to develop.

At the age of 68, my mother was diagnosed with pancreatic cancer. After recovering from surgery, her health improved enough for her to be able to visit my brother, her daughter-in-law and her five beloved grandchildren at their ranch in Goodland, Kansas. She also created eight more paintings during this time, which were the capstone to her life.

This period of respite was followed by six months of severe physical, spiritual, and emotional suffering. My mother and her sister Hedi remained very close throughout their lives, and Aunt Hedi was ever present during the last months of my mother's life. It was during this time that my mother met with Marsha Rossiter and decided to entrust to her the publication of this story. She passed away on May 29, 2009. At her request, her ashes were strewn on a hill overlooking my brother's home in Kansas.

As for me, well, her suffering was in the milk I nursed. I have never experienced hunger or homelessness or war. Still, the course of my life was altered by it. The experience of my mother and Aunt Hedi most definitely is not a one-generation happening. I have had a wonderful education and many opportunities in life. While not all have come to fruition, a faith in a loving God has prevailed and life has opened to me in many, many ways. That faith was planted in me and nurtured in me by my mother, *meine Mutti*.

It is with deep faith that I commend this work to each person who may chance to read it.

In His Name,
Susan Klemm Slaughter, Hildie's Daughter

Epilogue 3: Kenneth

*T*oday I received in the mail a duplicate birth certificate that I recently ordered from Illinois. I needed this to obtain a passport for an upcoming business trip. There, near the bottom, was my mother's signature. I marveled that her signature hadn't changed much in the past fifty years, even though I knew she had changed tremendously in that time.

The signatory was a 23-year-old citizen in a land she wasn't native to, and she was my mother. She was a model type of beauty, and I was her firstborn in this new land. She and my father gave me a name that sounded as American as possible — Kenneth.

My mother always had a great love for America and an abiding sense of gratitude for the peace and freedoms she enjoyed here. Even though it was, and still is, fashionable to be down on America in many of the circles my mother gravitated to, I never once heard her disparage this nation that had given her so much.

As a child of the sixties, I unfortunately adopted some of this anti-American tone, and I have vivid memories of my mother lovingly pointing out, "Yes, there are some problems here in this country, but it is still a wonderful place. Go out and fix the problems", she would say. My mother truly thought that if I so chose, I could become president of the United States — she understood what it was to be an American.

While she thoroughly enjoyed the peace and safety of her new life in the United States, she carried with her many emotional scars from her childhood war experiences. I remember when a new restaurant opened, not too far from our home in Chicago. It had the theme of a box car and lots of kids joked at school that it would never make it because none of the Jews in the neighborhood would eat there. When I related this to my mother, she confided in me that she would never eat there either, as the memories of the terrifying box car rides made her uncomfortable to even drive by it. The school-boy humor left me rather quickly as I reflected on the seriousness of my dear mother's tone. The horrors of war suddenly seemed not so distant and surely no longer funny.

The war years were never spoken of in our home. My parents never shared their memories of what they had witnessed and experienced. This brief conversation gave me the first inkling that my mother was not like the mothers of my friends.

Much later in life, I moved my family to a ranch in Kansas. I maintained a small office in the nearby town and my mother loved to visit me at the office when I worked there. I think she loved to see that yes, in America, if you work hard, you can succeed. Even a kid from the city can become a successful rancher who conducts transactions with customers coast to coast. One day, as we sat in my office at noon, the tornado sirens went off. In Kansas, the heart of tornado country, this is done as a regular test and everyone knows it is just a test. Some folks even set their watch by it.

My mother panicked. Her countenance changed from happiness to extreme worry — an almost uncontrollable panic. She asked what the sirens were for and I explained they were just a test. It took me a bit to understand what was happening. My mother was reliving the experience of being bombed, and the sirens were the soundtrack of a terrible part of her youth. She quickly left and went back to the ranch. Later, she confided in me that she could never live in a town that had tests such as these. Mom's life was very different than others.

With the wisdom of middle age, I now see that my mother had a choice in life. The experiences she survived could have driven her to live a life of fear or anger or aggression or hopelessness or self-destruction. Instead, she chose love, peace, caring, and self-betterment. Her choice made all the difference in my life, and for that, I am eternally grateful.

My mother's love for me and for my sweet wife and our five wonderful children has set an example for each of us. She gave of herself to us over the years in such unselfish and caring ways that she truly left her mark on our hearts. In so doing, her life will echo throughout the generations. When I read of Christ's unconditional love, the only earthly example I have of this is the love of my mother. She has given all of us that great gift. Ironically, I credit her dedication to this path to the awful things she witnessed and lived through as a child. A good mother wants to shield her children from all the bad she has had to endure and my mother put her all into her job!

As I grew older, I became more aware of the emotional scars my mother carried and I longed to somehow help her overcome them. Regrettably, I was mostly ineffective as my understanding of her experiences was not sufficient. I suspect many who loved her have had this same problem.

It was no small task for my mother to relive her war time experiences so others could read these words. This book was one of her proudest accomplishments. I am now old enough to begin to understand why.

Mom had the courage to go back to the war and recall those terrible experiences in detail great enough to put them on paper. I believe her motivation for this was to inspire readers to see the horrors of war through the eyes of a child. I know she hoped that her writing would lead to a more peaceful world. She often echoed Christ's words from His Sermon on the Mount: "Blessed are the peacemakers for they shall be called the children of God." She strove to be a peacemaker, and this book is a fruit of that effort.

Perhaps this book was also a way to put those experiences to rest and to allow those of us who did not fully understand her to get a deeper insight into who she was.

It is my feeling that she succeeded on both counts. When I read the first draft many years ago, I instantly understood many things about my mother that had escaped me until then. Mom's book was the catalyst that softened the log jam of pent-up memories in our extended family, too. After this book, other stories began to slowly, painfully emerge. The healing process began in earnest and continues to this day.

It is my hope that readers of this work will carry on the lessons learned from a brave, honest, and loving woman. Love deeply, use restraint, seek after peace in all things. And always, always remember the children. A child's eyes are not like those of an adult. Children know not when to look away, and what goes in goes straight to the soul. Christ taught: "Suffer little children to come unto me... for of such is the kingdom of God."

May God Be with You Always,
Kenneth Joseph Klemm, Hildie's Son

Hildie Weiler's Photo Album

Hedi and Hildie c. 1940-41

Kathe, Hildie, Hedi c. 1940-41

Westermeyer home, Miletitsch

Jakob Weiler butcher shop, Zombor c. 1933

Hedi, passport photo

Hildie, passport photo

Joseph Westermeyer, Hedi, Hildie, Kathe,
onboard the *Ernie Pyle*, 1946

Hildie, Kathe, Hedi at the Schultz
farm in Illinois, 1946

Hildie and Hedi, teenagers in
Chicago, c. 1956

Hedi and Hildie , 2007

www.ingramcontent.com/pod-product-compliance
Lightning Source LLC
Chambersburg PA
CBHW031156270326
41931CB00006B/291